"The quality of permanency in a transient world is terrifying."

James Stephens (1882-1950) "The Triangle"

A QUART JAR OF PEACHES

Other works by John J. Mahoney

The Year

Summer Tides & Cinnamon Thyme

Symphony of Seasons

Wine of the Muse

Every Bottle has a Story

Mystic Isle

Wine for Intellectuals

Wine: The Source of Civilization

A QUART JAR OF PEACHES

JOHN J. MAHONEY

DUBLIN NEW YORK MILMAY

The poetic essay, "Milmay", Chapter 3-A, was previously published by The Mitre Press, London, England in 1976 as part of *The Wine of the Muses*, by John J. Mahoney. Its inclusion here is an edited version.

John Mahoney can be reached through e-mail at j.mahoney@juno.com

First printing by CreateSpace, a division of Amazon, January 21, 2020

ISBN: 978-171058329-8

3 5 7 9 8 6 4

For my granddaughter Madeline Olivia Ortiz and grandson Kai Beckett Mahoney. May Madeline, with her older brother Liam, and Kai, with his older sister Cameron, find pleasure in their later years from the memories of their youth, and everyone else who reads this book; both young and old.

ACKNOWLEDGEMENTS

The review reading, editing typo mistakes, and verbal positive encouragements from Louann Wittman, an academic scholar who insists that all her students learn to think more deeply, have made the publication of this novel possible. She is one of the most dedicated teachers I've ever known, and as a former colleague, I am indebted to her for sharing her literary wisdom. She taught students to think. She helped her peers to do their best, and called on them to share their knowledge with her students as she has shared her knowledge with me. I sincerely thank you, Louann.

Thank you also to John Gartland who read the first chapter very early on, and made suggestions that have all been incorporated into this novel. I know of no other person, besides my wife Joanne, who reads more and grows intellectually every single day. His help and friendship are a treasure.

And also to Earl Wester, a college roommate from half a century ago who dislikes and views commas as speed bumps to reading. He looked up all 72,266 words of this novel. "Wes," thank you for having never changed.

Je vous remercie, grazie, ευχαριστώ, gracias, danke, 감사합니다, *obrigado, and thank* you to all the members of the Dionysian Society, International who have read my wine reviews and other books, and continue to encourage me to write more. I have. Please share this work with your own friends, and also share their comments.

A QUART JAR OF PEACHES

1

Amor vincit omina, the ancient Latin phrase, is certainly true; yes, love can indeed conquer all, but death changes everything, and can even keep a young boy from ever feeling like, or even being twelve again. While eating the last jar of peaches my mother had prepared for a winter dessert, a few years after her passing, I recalled being immortal during the summer of 1956.

When I was twelve years old, I was more than Prince of the grapevines, Count of the Chicken Coops, and Duke of the Barn; I was King of Milway. That was a long, time ago in a land far, far away from the modern world. The middle of the Twentieth Century was filled with a special kind of magic every minute of every day, and I was certain that it would go on forever.

I loved the first day of summer. It only became summer when school was out, and our two teachers, Mrs. Sneely and Clara De Ross, were far from our minds. Our summer had nothing to do with any Solstice measurement; it meant freedom. The two teachers of the two-room, multi-class Milway schoolhouse were out of sight and out of mind, and the more often we got out of our houses and played among ourselves, the better our mothers liked it. Freedom's just a synonym for no responsibility. Billy Strusser and I were free.

He was also twelve years old, and he was my next-door neighbor. A little older were Ricky, Anthony, and Leo, whom we all called Tudor; they too were free. Dominic was too old to be totally free, but his younger brother Sammy, and my older brother Jimmy were kind of free, but all three of them had the restraints of being much older. High school eradicated their full freedom, and even took away some of their memories of what totally *free to just be*, really was.

Those of us who lived right in the center of Milway were the core of the town's fraternity, the Lords of Milway, the Knights of summer's mystical realm. During the school year, we saw and played equally with all the girls during recess, but during the summer, it was almost always just a small group of boys who banded together, and made the endless days of the summer's activities the foundation for all of our future endeavors and relationships. Summer. Time could let it be endless if He wanted it to be. Milway summers were never to be forgotten, but one unique summer taught me the most. During the summer of 1956 I learned what only our species knows for certain. Among all the other animals on earth, we alone are burdened with knowing something that Time teaches, and I, like everyone else, had to learn to accept it

In 1956, I was twelve years old. That's the best age that you can ever be. No doubt about that, even if you live to be well over a hundred. Twelve. It's when you stand alone in complete control of every day's activities, and when you are at the center of the complete universe.

Lettuce had already been harvested, and strawberry picking was coming to an end, but my buddy Billy and I would still scour the already-harvested strawberry rows in the field behind my house to pick and savor the forgotten berries. They may have been too green at the time, or just skipped over while hiding under a leaf, but now they were perfect. Few things in life can beat a freshly picked ripe, red strawberry to savor on your young tongue. A few years later, my Aunt Florence and my Uncle Joe would build a house in that field behind my backyard, and my cousins, Joanne and Joey, would live there in solitude never knowing of the adventures that took place on the land just below and around their home. That Uncle Joe was just Joe, he and his Army Company were among the first Americans to cross the Rhine River and enter Germany near the end of the Second World War. My other Uncle Joe was called Popeye, just like in the comics. He fought against the Germans too, but in North Africa. He never married, taught me how to put in an electrical fuse box, and how to remove summer ticks without leaving part of their head stuck in you. He taught important stuff.

It was a Monday morning when my buddy Billy Strusser and I ventured into the woods just beyond the strawberry field to find and clear a spot for a summer fort. We built lots of forts. Just about twenty-five yards into the woods, we started clearing the dead leaves and underbrush away on a location surrounded by some enormous white oaks. By lunchtime, we had a spot that would keep us tick-free when we played or camped out there. We'd cut back the underbrush, rake away the dead leaves, and have a camping site or a perfect area to build a new fort. It was Time who scattered the dead, brown leaves all around trying to remind us that summer doesn't last forever, but we knew better. We alone could make it last forever, and that particular summer we planned on doing it.

"I'll get our small sledgehammer right after lunch, Billy said, "and you get those railroad spikes we found along the tracks." We'd explore along the railroad tracks that split the town in two at least once a week nearly all year long. The railroad ran right through the center of Milway, and cut the town exactly in half. We'd pick up and keep whatever we found discarded along the rails.

"Okay," I answered. "Right after you eat, meet me back here."

"Okay, right here."

By the time Billy came back that afternoon, I still hadn't found where I'd hidden the spikes knowing that they might be used in some future endeavor, but I did find an old bicycle tire inner tube. Forgetting about the spikes we wanted to use at our new fort for a while, we adjusted our plans, and cut the rubber tube up into thin eight-inch strips to make slingshots. Summer had really begun as soon as you built or, quite honestly, as soon as you made something. Summer is when you're endlessly active.

We knew we'd have to hike back into the woods and seek out two perfectly shaped young tree limbs that branched off into a "Y" for our slingshots. I was pretty good with a slingshot; not so with Billy. I had a knack of how high to shoot a small rounded stone so that it could fall into the center of a target. Planning ahead was the key to being good at things. Billy got close to targets, but seldom ever hit them dead center. I never saw Anthony use one, but his brother Ricky was very good at hitting targets with his slingshot. Tudor would use my slingshot, but he had no interest in making one for himself. Ricky and I were known to be quite good, maybe the best, at using them, but there was a younger kid over in Richmount, the first town west of Milway, named Eddie who was best shot anywhere. He was known all over for his acute skills in firing a slingshot. He must have collected the best round stones. He had some cousins in Milway, and everyone had heard about this Eddie's slingshot skills. We had all heard that he never missed. The rounder the stone you use when firing a slingshot, the straighter it flies toward your target. Ricky and I knew that to be true, but other guys in our gang would pick up any old stone, and try to make it hit their target. They all missed far more often than we ever did. I bet that Eddie kid must have used marble-round stones to be as good a shot as we'd heard him to be.

I took a hatchet and a hand saw from my Uncle Mike's garage, and then Billy and I scurried across the strawberry rows back to the spot we'd cleared that morning. Mike's real name was Walter; his brother George was Foxy, Uncle Joe was Popeye; all of the post-Depression people that I was related to seem to have gotten nicknames from the characters in the Sunday funnies. Popeye had fought against Rommel in North Africa. Foxy had been in the Navy. He had to be rescued from a sunken submarine in the North

Atlantic. There was even a World War I veteran in Milway named Clarence Monteith who had flown Bi-planes over France, and was now a cracker-jack mechanic for Bullkey Chevrolet in Vineland, a town twelve miles away. All our parents shopped there, but to me, Vineland was a far-away country. Milway had everything I needed.

As soon as we entered the woods, Billy saw a small tree and found his idea of the ideal limb right away. He cut the first limb he saw that branched off into the Y shape that we needed to make a slingshot. It wasn't quite symmetrical, but it would work. I've always been more meticulous in my endeavors, so I spent half an hour seeking out the ideal, necessary shape to make a perfect slingshot. When I finally spotted the perfect Y-shaped branch, it was ironically in the same tree that Billy had cut his from thirty minutes earlier. It was just higher up than where he'd cut, and only noticeable from a distance. I sawed the handle about five inches below the Y split, and then cut the two limbs about four inches up each side above what would be my biblical weapon's handle. I now had the perfect piece for a slingshot. I had no idea that the famous David of the Bible story used an entirely different type of sling.

We were pleased to find and eat a few strawberries still surviving in the already harvested strawberry patch as we ambled back toward the workshop in the garage. There was also another shop, a blacksmith's shop in part of the barn where I'd bend iron, and straighten old bent nails with my grandfather, but for this job, we needed the newer shop.

We cut the tire tube strips about half an inch wide, as we'd done before, and once again they were too hard to pull and stretch. The half-inch strips of bicycle tire inner tube are just too thick. The best strips for slingshots are about three-eights of an inch wide. Why we didn't learn that faster is beyond me, but over those youthful years we always cut the rubber tire tube strips too wide on our first attempts every single time we tried to make new slingshots. My father used to say, "Measure twice and cut once," so you didn't make a mistake measuring and then ruin a good piece of lumber. Maybe that's why I figured I can always cut it thinner, but if it was too thin to start, I couldn't make it wider. I remember thinking I hope that's the reason for always making a mistake on the first cut. It's either that, or I was just too dumb to remember how to do it correctly.

We wrapped each strip around the top of the Y, and stapled it together and onto the uppermost part of each side of the Y-shaped limb. We tied the other ends to a small square of canvas we cut from a cover we found over a garden pump. In a magical land like Milway, you could find everything you ever needed to build weapons, campsites, or castles. Yes, in 1956, Milway was magical.

On our way out of the garage's shop, I spotted the railroad spikes that we'd been looking for earlier. We took what we'd need for making the tree steps outside, but left them in the grass to pick up later on as we searched for small rounded stones to use as we broke in our new slingshots. We each fired nearly a dozen stones, pulling each shot further back, and seeing the stones fly faster and further toward the old barn. By our sixth shot, we knew the rubber strips, which had been finally cut to just about three-eights of an inch wide, would hold together and work well. We were now the two most dangerous characters in our make-believe army of Knights who were seeking out Ogres that had invaded our kingdom. We shot at corn stalks, maple trees in the yard, and at the wooden door of the old corn bin shouting out that those objects must have been the hideous, legendary man-eating monsters.

The new slingshots held our attention for the rest of the afternoon. Driving the railroad spikes into a lookout tree above where our new fort would be would just have to wait until the next morning. Minutes, hours, even days mean nothing during the freedom of summer.

My Uncle Foxy had told me that back around World War I, about 1918, there was a cast iron slingshot called Zip-Zip. He also told me he had a 1946 copy of a magazine called Popular Science, and in it was an article about how to made the perfect slingshot. White birch and ash wood were the best, but in reality, any strong limb that grew into a Y-shape, could be used. Billy and I used our slingshots like catapults and fired mostly at poles or trees imagining them to be castle turrets or invading monsters.

I rushed through breakfast the next morning. My mother asked, "Why are you eating so fast. Slow down. You'll get cramps."

"We're building a fort, and Billy's waiting for me," I answered.

"Where?" she asked.

"On the edge of the woods past the strawberry field."

"Don't get hurt," she replied with a parental tone that gave me absolute freedom to explore, and play whatever I wanted, "and watch for ticks," she added, and then concluded, "and don't get hurt."

I can recall her adding, "Don't get hurt," to just about everything she ever said to me after I explained what I was planning for the day. I heard my friends' mothers say the same thing so I assumed that all mothers everywhere tell their kids to not get hurt. Maybe they thought we planned to hurt ourselves on purpose. In any case, "Don't get hurt," is a universal maternal decree!

It had gotten quite warm now, and the start of summer was filled with sunny blue skies nearly every day. All the rainy days during April where just a fading memory. The early summer green had more of a lime hue to it, and every new tree, lilac and hedge leaf was in perfect shape. As any summer continues, the lime-green fades into a darker duller blue-green, and many of the leaves slowly become disfigured. I first noticed that when I was just a little kid. By the time I turned twelve that information was just taken for granted and I was sure that everyone was well aware of the changes.

We could do almost anything we wanted to do. We were free to fall down, scrape our knees, and free to get dirty. Grass stains, dirt in our ears, and torn pants were things that just happened everyday. We learned to live with the problems presented to us by the risks we took. Knee scrapes and small cuts on your fingers did not constitute "getting hurt".

I drank down the remainder of my Rice Krispies right from the bowl, and rushed off to find Billy. Milk always tasted special and unique after it had soaked up the flavor from all the Rice Krispies swimming in it. Of course when I got to Billy's house, I had to wait another half an hour while his mother questioned him about our plans for the morning. He had the same freedoms I had, but he had to go through a more intense interrogation than I ever did. My mother had more work to do, I guess, so she couldn't drill me with as many questions because she simply didn't have as much time. Besides, whatever we had planned would usually change as soon as we stumbled on to, or discovered something new.

"When you hear the siren," she told Billy, "get back here quickly for lunch."

"Sure will, Mom," Billy answered her.

"Let's go," I said to Billy.

"Don't get hurt," warned his mother.

The siren at the Milway firehouse blew everyday at noon back then, and it still does today. I assumed it sounded off for Adam and Eve too. Some things have just always been there. It signaled noontime years before I was ever born. I think it was to let the factory workers, at the now abandoned canning plant, know when to break for lunch. There was an old tomato canning company that used to employ dozens of people long before even my older brother was born. I heard from my Uncle Mike that once the Depression started, it closed down never to reopen. Now, it was just a dark mysterious labyrinth of adventure filled with old cans still on the bottling lines, and dozens of other curious prehistoric items like labels, posters, and tin caps for the cans.

Billy and I set off for the woods. New Jersey's state tree is *Quercus ruba*, the Northern Red Oak, but Milway was filled mostly with White and Black Oaks. There were wild Dogwoods, Pitch Pines, the pine that covers our famous Pine Barrens section of the state, and Tulip trees, but the sixty-foot White Oak, the *Quercus alba*, was our target. Its white-gray flaking bark made it look whiter than all the other trees except the few white birch trees that grew in more open areas. The oak's limbs spread out making a full umbrella. Its leaves were a dark green on top, and more of a lime green underneath. When my grandfather cut and split it for firewood, the opened sides turned a pale yellow color; it's the wood you see on many floors. The strong smelling Pitch Pines interspersed among the oaks, is the wood they used for railroad ties because it contains so much resin. The pine resin helps to preserve it for a very long time. My mother had a bottle of liquid stuff in our kitchen that smelled like the Pine trees. She cleaned our floors with it. I bet it came from the Pitch Pines.

Well, I already had the railroad spikes waiting in a bucket, and Billy carried the small sledge taken from his garage. We quickly picked the largest White Oak tree at the location where we started clearing the day before, and immediately began to drive in the first railroad spike. It would serve as the first step so that we could climb up to where the limbs forked out. There, we'd build a lookout platform so we could protect our future fort from every imaginary enemy. The spikes were eight inches long. We figured that if we drove the spikes in about four inches that would leave us another four inches to step on as we climbed up the great White Oak.

It took nearly two hours to drive in just one railroad spike. They were three-quarters of an inch thick. The spikes were the enormous nails they used to attach the iron rails down onto the railroad ties. We pounded them only halfway into each side of the oak tree. No one could have ever paid us enough money to do that as a job, but it was the start of summer. We were free. Even Time ignored us. So, we labored like Egyptian slaves. We'd need an open place to pitch a tent to sleep in the wilds of what we called the wilderness, even though you could see both our houses from the clearing in the woods. We seldom thought far ahead of the moment we were living in. Staggered spikes on each side of the tree. Little by little we went up, and after the third one was driven in, we decided that we'd only work in the cooler mornings. The afternoon heat got to be too much for us. Slingshot practice, and make-believe hunting games occupied our afternoons. The real reason might have been that our arms were too weary to swing the sledge even one more time. We were young boys doing grown men's work.

*   *   *

The following day, we borrowed four old wooden potato crates from my grandfather's sweet potato storage building to stand on so we could swing the hammer as we went up with each new spike-step. My grandfather's sweet potato house was across the street from my home. It wasn't used for anything until September and October's harvest, when it would become filled with sweet potatoes to be sold during the frosty winter. The aromas in there were magnificent; sweet potato first, then, when it mixed with the smoke from the wood-burning stove that kept the potato harvest from freezing until they were all sold, a different mixture of aromatics saturated both your clothes and your nose. My parents, and my aunts and uncles, always knew if I'd been playing in the sweet potato house during winter because of how I smelled.

In summer, the aromas were quite different, and I quickly learned to distinguish subtle differences found in the same building at different times of the year. We learned a lot because we all paid attention to the sights, sounds, smells, and textures of all the things we played with. By the time we were twelve, we didn't taste as many things as we used to taste when we were just little kids. I hadn't put a bug or a worm into my mouth since I was five. That was an earlier time in our lives when everything we touched and smelled also went into our mouths. We'd out grown doing that by now, well, at least most of the time.

We each carried two crates out of the building. They would become our scaffold so we could drive the spikes into the tree way above the ground. After another day and a half, the last spike went in, we both climbed up to where we planned to build a lookout tree hut, but our interest waned, and it was never completed. The energy it took to do all this work also diminished our enthusiasm for the project. We did, however, camp out there a number of times, sleeping under the spreading oak, where the mosquitoes held a feast on us. By the third time we slept in our safe area among the jungles of the forest, as we called it, we knew we'd better search for another summer quest. The rainy spring had increased the mosquito population, and they finally got the better of us. We were ready and able to fight off Indians and Viking warriors, but we were beaten by the bugs.

Billy said that he had broken his slingshot the weekend after we started the fort project, and I think I left mine in the potato house where it wouldn't be found until nearly Christmas by an uncle who thought best not to return it to me for my own good. We'd need new slingshots if we were to survive a summer filled with invading enemies of every sort. So once again, we cut bicycle tire inner tubes, ventured into the woods to find perfect Y-shaped limbs, cut them, and attached the new rubber straps. Once again, we could feel the safety of being armed in case of some make-believe enemy's invasion. We had become master slingshot makers instead of craftsmen who built wooden forts.

Over the next six years, until I was a senior in high school, I'd often walk back into that wonderful forest and check in on our never completed fort to see all the spikes that we drove into that tall oak tree. I saw the spikes shrink into the tree as the wood slowly grew over them until one semester break during college, a life time later, I walked back to the clearing in the woods and saw only wooded bumps over where the spikes had been inserted. A decade of growth had hidden the spikes. But near the end of that summer of complete freedom, Billy and I took sandwiches out there with two bottles of Coke, and I took along half a jar, just a pint, of my mother's first preserves of this year's peaches. Half jars were for the present; full quarts were only for after dinner on icy winter days. Nothing I've ever tasted was sweeter. That's when I first noticed the difference in colors between the top, and the bottom of the oak leaves. Of course we talked about finishing the fort project including the lookout platform high in the oak every time we went back there, but Time was sitting along side of us, and He wanted us to move along to other endeavors before we grew any older.

It seemed that I had started that project long, long ago. Yes, I was Lord of the Land, but this was one domain I never conquered. We were both fortunate that neither of us ever got hurt swinging the sledge hammer, working while standing on a sweet potato crate scaffold that shook and rocked as we swung the sledge, or while climbing the slender limbs of the oak tree. We had no idea about just being lucky, and we also had no idea that crazy old Luck was related to Time, and was his brother. Goofy old Luck seemed to be able to do whatever He wanted to do, but Time always had the final say in each one of life's situations, and Luck always followed Time's decisions and commands. They both came from the same place, and were born on the same day nearly fourteen billion years ago when everything else was created.

1-A

Potato. Bike. Sandwich. Peaches. All words. Words were strange things, I remember thinking when I was twelve years old. You looked at these squiggly ink or pencil marks; just strange straight or curved lines and strange shapes. Your mind sees them as something called letters. There's twenty-six of them in English, but only twenty-four in Greek. I wonder why? You learn to make a noise for each one of those shapes, and when you put them all together, and then make all their sounds out loud, you say a word. Miraculous! Words. Each one of these words has a meaning; they stand for something off the paper page or modern computer screen, and they really represent something. All those snake-like lines, some straight, some curved, when put together, become the things we call words. Some stand for a person, a place, or a thing. Some tell you what was happening; they show action. Some expand or restrict the idea, but every one of those words means something. Some have the power to tell you if the event you're talking or reading about happened in the past, the present, or the future. It's absolutely unbelievable that they all just started as squiggly marks. Yes, we call the different shaped ink or pencil marks letters, and each letter represents a different sound. Amazing.

It scares me to recall how young I was when I first realized that we think with words. If we don't have the word for something, we can't think about it. There's no such thing as a purple glass mountain, but now that I've given you words for it, you can, for the first time ever, picture a purple glass mountain in your mind.

We put a bunch of those words together, and call it a sentence. All those ink marks together have made a statement about something, and since we know the words, we understand the concept, or the thing being talked about. We can think about it because we think with words. It's impossible to think about something if you don't have a word for it.

When I first started reading books, simple children's books, I would keep a ballpoint pen and an index card, which was usually my page marker, all together by my bed. I believe that I started doing that when I was ten, or eleven. Whenever I came to a word I didn't know, I'd print it down, and as soon as possible, I'd go to that most wonderful book in the world, the book that contains every philosophy, every theology, every scientific possibility, and all of history, art, and literature that exist; I'd page through my dog-eared dictionary. Every thought any one has ever had, or will ever have, can be found in that Merlin of a text. All you'd have to do is put the words together in the correct order.

Yes, we think with words.

Someone gets an idea in his head. He formed some letters into words, and those words become sentences. I'd see the squiggly marks he put on some paper, and then I put them together as words. Then, I put those words into a sentence or two, and the idea that was formed in his head is transferred into my head. Miraculous! His head can be a thousand miles away, but because of words, the words he wrote down, I now have the idea that he formed in his head inside my head. Yes, miraculous! The person may have had the idea and written it down even before I was born, maybe a thousand years ago, but the minute my eye sees the word and sends it to my brain, I can have the same idea he had centuries ago and a thousand miles away. It's just unbelievable. Words!

People in other countries have different sounds for their letters, but they too simply put those sounds together to make a word. Words linked together make a thought, an idea, or maybe ask a question. The more correctly the words are lined up in the sentence, the easier it is to understand. A person gets an idea in their mind, makes squiggly marks, formed into letters that result in a word, then print a bunch of those words, as a sentence, for a complete thought. A list of similar thoughts forms a paragraph, which is basically just expanding the thought. If you knew what those foreign shapes and sounds represented, you'd think with their words in their language. Arabic, Greek, Chinese. It's all the same. You'd think with those words.

As I grew older, read more, and listened to grownups talk, I learned more words, and was able to think about more and more things. We simply think with words. No doubt about it. Every time I looked at a dictionary, I realized just how little I knew, and it scared me.

Even now, I know we think with words, and that we should never stop learning, but during the heat of summer and being free from school, all a boy wants to do is run barefoot on wet grass. Run, and never stop running and then a bit later, he could bicycle even further away from home. Then bicycle all day. You weren't supposed to have to think in summer; just do.

*   *   *

When you're twelve years old, there is little thought of anytime in the past. It's hard to recall anything you might have done during the summer before the current one. When you're twelve, there is only now; no future, no long-term plans, and not even a thought about what it will be like when you're older. Your parents have never ever been young, and you will never be old. The sun rises and sets each day, but nothing changes. Young children, and very old people, do not like change. They have a lot more in common than you'd think.

Billy's older sister, Joanne, viewed us as annoying children, and his younger sister Barbara was much too young to join our gang. Ricky and Anthony's younger brothers, Phil and Jo-Jo, were also too young for most of our adventures, but Phil and my younger cousin Gary would many times join us in our escapades. Neil Saxing and the Balder boys were around, but not involved in any of our projects. Dexter lived a bit too far away to join in at everyday play, as did Anita Grossie, and Duane De Ross who both lived even farther from all the major activities of the Milway realm. Johnny Matzeo biked over to our kingdom once in a while, but his brother, Bobby, was older and always ignored us as Time had instructed him to do. We all played together in school, but not during the magic daylight hours of summer.

Summer meant being in a different world, and the older kids along with the very young, were alien to it. Everyone used the same vocabulary, but not everyone saw the magic of words.

For some strange reason, both the very young and the very old tell their ages the same way. You don't say you're six; no it's, "I'm six and a half, not six." Then again when you're eighty-seven and a half, you say, "I'm eight-seven…almost eighty-eight!" Everyone in-between simply states how many years he or she has lived. "I'm forty-one now," even if you'll be forty-two in just a month or in less time than that. It's still just forty-one.

My younger cousin, Billy Layzan, played sports with us, but his younger sister, Sandra, was never impressed with our antics. Jack Krokokos, and his older sister, Judy, were also a bit too far away to join us every day in worshiping the endless hours of the mystical summer. Carol Matweow was well protected from the roughhousing boys, and she seldom sought our company. Neither did Cheryl DeRoss. Neil Saxing was also already too old, but Dexter would bike the mile into the heart of town, and sometimes join our world of make-believe. You'd be proud to call every kid in Milway your friend. Because we all used so many of the same words, we all tended to have similar values, and we all seemed to think alike. It was words that bound us all together. Words can be like herbs as they can garnish a relationship. Some words are like sugar and they sweeten the feelings between people and at the same time some words can poison your mind. Many of these negative words infect your mind with opinions that can seldom be changed. It takes a dozen sugar words to counteract the resentment formed by poison words. Be careful with words.

*   *   *

It's funny now that the words of that summer, a time so very long ago, still linger in my head. Sure, the smells and sounds of summer flow in the streams of your mind forever, but words, like people's names, for instance, seldom linger on the stony banks of that memory river. There are few, very few, winter words dancing along the pathways of my mind. Snow, sled, ice, and maybe Christmas are etched on the cavern walls of your mind, but most of the words you use are summer words. During the summer, you weren't supposed to have to think at all during those breaks in our formal education, but the words of a summer long past still float easily in my mind, and intermingle with the limited thoughts from all the other seasons over each and every year I've known.

Being deprived of the words from summers past is the worst thing that can ever happen to a person.

2

Spitz was Dominic's, Sammy's, and Tudor's father, as well as Ricky's uncle. They lived upstairs in the same house that Ricky lived in, but they had an outside private entrance. Ricky and his brothers lived downstairs, and both families shared the wine that was made and aged in the cellar of the large white-shingled two-family house.

Tudor once dropped a cat from the top of the outside staircase to see if cats really do always land on their feet. He dropped it from his second story entrance. It did twist and land on its feet. Really, it did. I remember it like it was yesterday. The cat hit the sidewalk with the sound a pillow makes when you have pillow fights, and hit your buddy's head. The cat lay still on the sidewalk for what seemed like an eternity as we all stood in silent admiration of him not splattering into a thousand pieces. Slowly, it stretched its legs, then wobbled off the sidewalk onto the grassy yard where it once again stopped and just laid still. We quickly lost interest watching what looked like a drunken cat, and didn't think much about it until later that day, just before I had to head home to finish my newspaper route, when we saw the cat hunting mice along side the chicken coops. He's fine, we thought. I was the paperboy for the entire community of Milway houses that could be reached by bicycle, and had a responsibility to deliver the papers everyday except Sunday.

We all secretly wished Tudor had flung the cat out farther to land on the grass instead of on the concrete. A basketball net is ten feet high. The cat fell from nearly double that height. We don't think he ever caught another mouse, but he never stopped trying.

Tudor's oldest brother, Dominick, was already grown up, and he never became a part of our entourage. I was helping my mother one day in the Post Office that was in the big room just off our kitchen, when he came in and asked for a stamp. I took the nickel, and gave him the five-cent stamp. He licked it, and put it upside down on the envelope as he explained to me that it sent a hidden message saying, "I love you". He was so old that he already had a girl friend. The upside-down stamp, and the entire gesture meant nothing to me. He must have been nineteen, maybe twenty. I didn't want to ever get that old, and do strange things like putting stamps upside down on letters to girlfriends. I had castles to attack, fields to explore, and blueberries to pick so my mother could bake pies, strawberries to pick so that she could make them into preserves, and later in the summer, peaches to help pick so she could skin, heat, and seal them in Ball Mason jars to use for desserts during the icy barren winter months.

The highlight of many January and February evening meals was a small bowl of golden sweet peaches drowning in an amber liquor of sugar water. Each bite initiated a flashback to summer when we drove to East Vineland to pick three or four half bushels by ourselves instead of paying extra money for the bushels that were already picked in front of the farm stand. The best ones were harvested near the end of the growing season. My father and I would pick them to take home where my mother, Helen, would use her wizard-like power of transforming them into golden-amber gems encased in glass vials where they could live forever, or at least until we opened them.

Dominic's younger brother Sammy was my brother Jim's best friend. They did everything together, but they were already too old to join in with any of our gang's daily adventures.

Neither Jimmy nor Sammy would have ever participated in the feline experiment that we had conducted because neither of them could remember ever being just twelve. Time had already stolen the greatest memories they'd ever have.

The day after we proved that cats do indeed always land on their feet, Ricky and I set out to flatten some of the pennies that we found by the gas pumps at Spitz's Texaco station. That gas station was on the opposite side of the street from my home, and just about a one hundred-yard walk from my house. It was directly across the street from Billy's house. Everything interesting in Milway was very close by.

The pennies had become my main concern. Ricky and I had a plan. Since the Pennsylvania Railroad ran three, sometimes four trains down to the Jersey shore each day, we figured all we had to do was lay the pennies on the train tracks, and wait for a train to pass over them. We expected to see a copper penny squashed flat, and become as thin as paper after it had expanded to the size of a quarter. Who knows, maybe it would be as large as a paper-thin half dollar?

Most of the trains were switching to diesels then, but the most fascinating locomotives still burned coal. They pulled boxcars and open coal cars. The coal was for the electrical power plant down by the shore. The smoke streaming above the line of boxcars and over a long line of open-top cars loaded with jet-black pieces of coal was like a tornado flying by. The smoke flew backwards in a long moving line behind the engine. All the cars were all covered with a cloud of rich black puffy smoke. Many years later, I'd reminisce about that aroma when savoring an old Barolo wine from Northern Italy, or some really old French Bordeaux. It was a sight to never be forgotten, and an aroma that you'd never forget. When the wind blew from the west, it moved the smoke across the field between the tracks and my house, and settled on any clothes my mother had hanging out on a line to dry in the sun. She hated it when a coal burner did that, but I loved the smell it left on my T-shirts.

From my front porch to the railroad tracks was less than forty yards. Together, Ricky and I sprinted across the field that was planted with peppers at that time, to set out our five pennies expecting a train to fly by at any minute. After we set them on the closest rail, we went back up the dirt bank above the rail bed to wait. There, we sat on the grass no farther than ten or twelve yards from the tracks. We waited. We watched down the tracks. We might see it before we heard it coming. We talked about how we might sell the unique paper-thin pennies.

Then Ricky said, "Suppose the wheels slip on the pennies? Do you think it could slide off the track? We could go to jail."

"I doubt it," I answered with an unconvincing tone in my voice. Maybe it was possible. You only think of these things during summer time, the mystical season, when you're free to be, and you're so young that life itself comes to a standstill. Nothing moves or grows; nothing ever changes when you're that young.

"Hey, hear that," he bellowed.

"Yea, it's coming," I answered.

Many times we would lay across the railroad ties with our ears on one rail. You could hear or sense a train miles and miles away. It actually works. We saw it done on the *Lone Ranger* television show. The Indians knew that the rail conducted the sound, and the Cowboys learned the trick from them. My mother had one of the first televisions in Milway. It had a very small viewing screen for such a large box. Three years earlier, in 1953, Mrs. De Ross brought some students over to see the Inauguration of President Dwight D. Eisenhower. I was more impressed with the older kids all sitting in our small living room and being so quiet. I can recall Mr. Eisenhower standing in front of a cluster of microphones, but that's all I can remember. I do remember a lot more episodes of the *Lone Ranger* and *Flash Gordon* than anything President Eisenhower said.

Since we could already hear the approaching train with our ears in the air, we wouldn't dare to lie with our ears on the tracks. Without saying anything to Ricky, I sprinted down the bank to the pennies, and quickly grabbed four of them. I ran to the top of the dirt bank and sat in the pepper field watching the three-car passenger train sprint by.

Ricky said nothing until the train flew by. "Wow, that was close."

It wasn't really close. I was safely in the field without Luck interceding at all, and not at all close to the train as it sped by.

"How many did you get?" he asked, as we both ran down to see the remaining penny.

"I picked up four."

As I was answering, Ricky spotted the penny, still in perfect shape, lying on the stones between two of the railroad ties. It must have slid off, or was shaken off, by the vibrations before the iron wheels got to it. We hadn't caused a major disaster, but we failed in our experiment to flatten a penny.

Many times that summer, and always after we played baseball across the tracks over in the ball park next to the Kupenski Bar, which was owned and run by my uncle John, who was known as Squeak, we'd try again to flatten a penny. My Uncle John was called Squeak by all the men in Milway; he was another one of my mother's brothers with a comic book nickname. Ricky and I would leave a penny on the tracks while walking home. I'd check it out the next morning. There was always one evening train between the shore and Philly. Time and time again, I reported to Ricky, that the penny was found unharmed lying inside or outside the rail.

We finally decided to try leaving all five pennies, about a foot apart, on the rail and just hope they didn't cause the train to derail. One just had to be squashed paper-thin.

The next morning, maybe the hottest day thus far of what my father called a "Sahara summer", a day without a breath of air moving, was a day when even the birds chose to sit still leaving the azure blue sky spotless, a hot summer day that grownups refer to as stifling, but young boys just ignore, was going to be the day of our final try to squash at least one penny.

We knew a freight train carrying loads of coal down to the electric plant very near to the coastline in Marmora, which was on the mainland, west of Ocean City, and at the mouth of the Egg Harbor River, came by every Wednesday just before noon.

By eleven o'clock, we placed three pennies two feet apart on one rail, and the remaining two pennies, also two feet apart, on the other rail. It had to work this time. It just had to.

After days of working on this penny project, we finally, for the first time, studied each penny. One was so old we couldn't be sure what date was printed on it. The other four were all from the 1940's. Three had 1949 printed clearly on them, but one was from 1944, and for no special reason, making it the most special penny we had, it was set down last on the side with just two copper coins waiting to be metamorphosed into the most unique coins in the world. The 1943-penny was made out of iron; the only time that happened. Copper war shortage I guess, but it didn't matter because we didn't have any of the 1943's. Iron may never have crushed like copper would.

We settled in for the wait by climbing back up the railroad embankment, and sat alongside the first row of green bell peppers. A few were starting to turn yellow. Their harvest was near.

Crops, it seems, take ages to mature when you're twelve years old, and minutes feel like days passing by when my buddies and I had to wait. The rows of pepper plants looked like small tomb stones in an old graveyard. *Cloon na Morav*, my father once mentioned, the Meadow of the Dead, was the graveyard near where he played as a boy while growing up in Ireland.

My favorite time of the summer was when we were harvesting the peaches, but that time would be ages away from today. Time! Who understood it? Who knew that Time watched us in the woods, sat with us along side the railroad, and spied on us as we slept. Time was a demon. Time made us think that waiting for something took forever, when in reality Time flew by like a jet carrying us all along with him. Jimmy Durante sang that *Old Man Time* took away everything but love. It would take me another fifty years to comprehend those lyrics.

I was going to suggest that we pick and each eat half of one of the almost yellow bell peppers when Ricky exclaimed, "I hear it!"

Turning my attention down the tracks toward Richmount, north of Milway, I shouted, "Me too. I can hear it too." Our feelings must have been identical to what Doctor Frankenstein felt during his famous shadowy experiment when the lightning storm was just beginning.

Very soon we could see it was a long train with many coal and boxcars. We simultaneously started counting. We always counted the number of cars of every train that flowed by during the summer. We always counted every single car, excluding the engine, but including the caboose. My bedroom window looked out to the west, toward the railroad tracks, and the old vacant rooms of the faded white three-story Milway Hotel to the left of the intersection, and Kupenski Bar to the right. I counted every train that ever went by always hoping to break my record of seventy-seven cars. This one would not be a record breaker, but it was long. We began counting just as the engine roared past us, and began to change at least one or two of our pennies into what would be, unknown to us, worthless pieces of flat copper.

"Ten," shouted Ricky, and then lowered his voice again until he shouted, "Twenty."

By then, I was somehow one car behind his count so I kept my voice lower. I couldn't shout, "Thirty," when he was already at thirty-one.

""Forty!" Ricky bellowed. We could see the end of the train approaching so he shouted, "Forty-Five," leaving just three more railroad boxcars, and then a caboose.

Forty-nine cars should have done the trick. The weight of forty-nine railroad coal and boxcars was massive, and should have easily worked their magic for us.

Ricky said, "Wow, forty-nine cars. Longest I've ever seen." But he didn't know how long the train was that I had counted from my bedroom window, and because I was still one car behind his count, I changed the conversation to the pennies.

"Let's go get them!" I shouted.

We both heard the final whistle the train made as it approached the next crossing while it sped along side Tuckahoe Road heading south toward the village called, Dorothy, and then to the shore towns beyond.

I got to the rail first, picked up two of the five pennies about six inches from the rail. Nothing. Ricky found another one of the three lying on the inside of the rail. Disappointment echoed in our expressions. We skipped to the other rail. Both pennies were lying together on a tie inside the rail.

Ricky took out a dime from his pocket and held it out. I only had a nickel on me.

"Get those pennies," he said. Let's go to Malatina's and get two chocolate popsicles. "You use the pennies with your nickel, and you'll have enough." When it came to doing math for ice cream, we were all Einstein's. Getting the correct number of boxcars was more difficult.

I stared down at the pennies, especially at the 1944 one, and I knew immediately that we'd never again experiment with having trains crush coins into enchanted flat disks. We felt Time leap over us as we raced across the tracks, up the other side embankment, across Tuckahoe Road, and into Mrs. Malatina's small grocery convenience store.

She stopped dusting as we entered and walked toward us knowing we'd want something.

"Two chocolate popsicles, please" I politely said.

She kept an eye on Ricky as I spoke because kids were always stealing some penny candies. Without ever looking down, she reached into the box freezer, and with no effort at all, she presented two chocolate treats. We paid. She counted the pennies without ever knowing how close they had been to being changed into expensive collector's items, and said, "Eat slowly. They're frozen. You'll get headaches." She was still talking when we left the store.

We couldn't make out her final comments as we pushed our way through the screen door onto her front porch, and then walked back down to the railroad tracks where we each sat on opposite rails, and talked only about how great the ice cold fudge was on such a hot day.

The best fudge bar I ever had was at the Bronx Zoo in New York City. During our Easter break from school, my father took my mother and me up to New York for a quick visit to Uncle Packy's house. He hadn't seen him in about two years, so we made it a two-in-one excursion. We stopped at his house and had a lunch of coffee and cinnamon buns. Aunt May gave me some Coke instead of coffee. My New York cousins only drank coffee and smoked cigarettes. It seemed to me that that was all they did all the time, starting at breakfast, and then throughout the entire day. I recall thinking that if that's what city people do, I'm really glad to be living in Milway, even though the cinnamon buns were really great.

They lived above Fordham University, so it was easy to head south to the Bronx Zoo. My father said that it was the largest zoo in America. Philadelphia had the oldest zoo in America, but to a kid, being the largest was more important. It was the first time I ever saw real monkeys, and even real live lions. Sure, I'd seen pictures of them, and saw them on some television shows, but to hear the lions roar, and listen to the monkeys screech at each other, was wonderful. Even more than the sounds and the sight of all the animals, I remember the smells of the entire day. Wild animals smelled so much different than the dogs, cats, cows or horses I had living around me. Even the pigpen behind my Grandfather's couldn't compare to the scent of the real live lion.

For weeks after that visit to the Bronx Zoo, I'd make monkey screeches when we played in the woods. After I described it all to Billy, he too would keep a lookout for lions and monkeys when we played at being explorers visiting the Congo. We both loved that word: *Congo*. It was musical and mysterious all at the same time. We both loved movies or television shows that took place in the jungle. Jungle is a very musical word; it sounds like you're singing when you say it, but Congo was my favorite word for a long time.

I hated long auto trips as a kid, but the safari to the Bronx Zoo was worth it, even if I had to get carsick once again. That was something that almost always happened to me. Before we left the zoo that special spring day, my father bought me an icy fudge bar while my mother said that I'd probably throw it up on the way home. I took one lick, then a small bite, and knew it was the best fudge bar I'd ever had. I didn't care if it would increase the odds of making me carsick. If it did make me carsick, I figured I'd get to taste it again. It was great being so young and always looking at the bright side of everything.

*   *   *

Ricky was always a big help when I had ideas for experiments, and he would soon help me again when we decided to dig a cave, and have a place for cooling off when midsummer became unbearable for all the guys in our gang, and also unbearable for every Milway adult. For now, I had already decided to get Billy first thing the next morning, and give our fort one last try. We didn't really need the lookout platform up in the giant oak; we could just build a tepee as a fort. Playing cowboys and Indians was always one of our most popular activities. The tepee was just another possibility if it didn't feel just right about building a larger fort. Everything we did had to be in sync with the natural world around us. We were just a very small part of a much bigger picture, and we all were well aware of it. Things have to be in sync. Old Time's first cousin, Chance, knew that too.

3

The next morning was a sizzling summer Saturday, but how many twelve-year-olds have ever let a hot summer's day prevent them from doing what they had planned? The answer is none. I, and all the local guys, would probably play some baseball later that afternoon, just before sunset when it cooled off a bit, but I had the entire morning to get Billy, pick up and collect, or cut a number of smaller trees, and then build our tepee-style-fort along side our spiked oak tree.

We had gotten the idea of making steps with spikes from seeing the big nails they put into telephone poles so a lineman could easily get up to where he might have to fix something. Those nails were about a foot long, and stuck out of each pole at least six inches, making them safer than what we had in our oak tree. Those spike steps gave Lineman a ready-made ladder whenever they needed it. We too had planned to have access to climbing up a tree to get to a lookout platform. No enemy army would ever be able to sneak up on us. We'd spot Black Knights, Indians, or Nazis before they ever got close to us. We pushed the lookout platform further back on our list of necessary things to do. Getting all the long sticks for our tepee-fort now became our primary concern.

Billy lived right next door to my house. The barn, with its attached shop where my grandfather worked, was right next to my house, and past that was a scale house. Coal bins were running back from the road, all the way to where the corn bin was located, and just beyond that, was the tomato field. Different sizes of coal were in each one of the bins. My uncle Mike would weigh the truck at the scale house, then load coal onto the dump truck. Then, he re-weighed the now-loaded truck to know how many tons of coal were in it. That was the only way he'd know how much to charge. You paid by weight, a ton or a half-ton. Subtracting the weight of the empty truck from the weight of the full truck told him how much coal was in it. It wasn't school, but it was an exercise in logic. I helped him with loading the coal, and adjusting the scale. I even did the subtractions for him, and it all took place during the time when so many people began making the change from coal stoves to oil heaters.

I'd ride with him to the houses in a place called Bear's Head, toward Ways Cove, where few people had changed from coal to oil as yet. I was sent down into their cellars to receive the coal, line up a coal chute from their coal pile, up through a basement window, and onto the rear of the dump truck. Uncle Mike would then slowly dump the ten-million-year-old material down into their cellars. A cascade of shiny ebony rocks would provide the warmth they'd need once the marvelous summer had scurried off with autumn into the cold darkness of winter.

It sounded like a landslide. Slowly at first, then with the speed of cataracts on a fast flowing river, the grapefruit-sized chucks of coal rumbled down the chute, and fell onto the concrete floor like a midnight hailstorm attacking an old tin roof. I hated all the coal dust, but I loved the roaring sound as the coal hit the cellar floor.

The dust it made coated my hands and face. I'd become a black boy. I had learned very early on that we're all really the same under the different shades of our skins. Little did the dinosaurs know that the limbs and leaves they compressed as they walked the earth they ruled, would one day provide the heat to help us survive the freezing winters of the future. It wasn't very long into my future that everyone stopped using coal, but Chance put me in the right place at the right time. She made sure, at least, that I got to experience a survival ritual, the storing of coal for the winter furnace that few, if any, people will ever have to do again.

Behind the coal bins was a twelve-foot tall row of hedges marking the divide between our workspace places, and the Strusser's well-manicured yard and home. At the far end of the hedgerow, was a corn bin: eight feet wide and twelve feet long with its cedar shingled roof about ten feet above the ground. It was usually full of corn by late August or September, but it was empty now. Beyond the corn bin, was a half-acre tomato field running back to the woods where we were about to start working on, and quickly complete a tepee-fort that we'd use for the remainder of the summer.

I'd meet Billy at the corn bin. Then, we'd track through the rows of some red, but mostly still orange-green tomatoes or totally green tomatoes, and leave civilization by entering the forest beyond the field. This garden would also disappear the following year when my Uncle Joe and Aunt Florence built their house on the property. My mother was one of ten children, and Florence was two years older than the youngest girl in the family, my Aunt Pauline. Both of these youngest sisters worked for the county government for as long as I could remember. There were five boys and five girls in my mother's house when she was growing up. It was the house across the street where my grandparents lived. Her oldest sister, Mary, left to get married when she was just seventeen, so my mother had to quit school when she was just in sixth grade to help my grandmother take care of all her younger brothers and sisters. That's the way it was back then. Everyone simply did what had to be done. No questions asked. I don't think there have ever been stronger people than those who lived through the Great Depression and then the Second World War. Nope, none stronger.

The education she got, however, was good enough for her to be able to learn how to correctly do all the government bookkeeping when she became the Milway Postmaster, a position she worked at for forty-two years. Schools back then taught you to think on your own, provided a lot of math and reading skills, and if you were at all intelligent like she was, you could master whatever you needed to survive. In all her decades of doing the federal government's accounting work, she was off by only four cents, just once, about three years before she retired. Milway was filled with amazing people.

*　　　*　　　*

Ricky and Anthony were heading toward Malatina's store when Billy and I saw and yelled to them. Maybe we'd get some help with our new fort.

Anthony had little desire for physical labor, but Ricky made him join us in the tomato field. We all sat down in the same row, on the soft dirt, half way into the field, while Ricky talked about our penny experiment with the trains. Billy and Anthony seemed to be deeply interested to hear about it. Ricky then said something he hadn't mentioned at all when the two of us were at the railroad.

"Yea, " he started. "It was like we were being watched. I could feel something first pushing me toward the tracks, then pulling me back away from them as the train approached."

"You're nuts," his brother said.

"Maybe not," interjected Billy. "I sometimes get that feeling when I'm waiting for something, or even waiting for somebody."

"Yea, it happens when I'm waiting," Ricky added.

"You're both nuts," said Anthony, but he was a little older than the rest of us, and may have already lost the ability to sense or be aware of some of summer's magic. I didn't interject anything about Time being around us always pushing us toward something, or pulling us back into somewhere; somewhere that only He knew was the place for us.

"Hey, this one's sweet," said Anthony as he bit into the almost-red tomato he had just picked from the plant behind him. "Try one."

We all took for granted the abundance of summer foods stored or growing around us in the cornucopia of Milway. We had to search for ripe, red ones, but soon, all four of us were munching on our own reddish ripe tomato, and talking with our mouths full about playing baseball later that afternoon.

That's just about when the tomato fight began.

Billy threw one at me and just missed my head. We instantly backed apart, crossing rows, ducking red and still yellowish projectiles, and surveying for more ammunition, more ripe tomatoes. In less than a full minute, a major tomato war had broken out. Spontaneity is something that fades away, along with the years, as you age.

Splat! My pitch caught Ricky in the chest.

Wam! Anthony's landed dead-on Billy's shoulder. He had tomato juice on the side of his cheek and on his hair.

Zoom! One went flying by Anthony's head. He turned and ran back toward the corn bin. Billy ran toward the woods as I backed away toward the strawberry patch. I stopped throwing when Billy stopped. Each of us had at least one red stain on our white T-shirts. Tiny tomato seeds and red juice slid slowly down our sides. By then, Anthony was past the corn bin and heading home by cutting through Strusser's back yard. Ricky, who was among the better baseball players, not only on our team of local players, but also better than everyone in Milway School, and he could throw further than anyone I knew. He reached down and picked a hard green tomato, and then he fired it into the sky toward his brother. Unfortunately, Anthony, at the same time, turned back toward us to wave goodbye. We knew he didn't want to help cut trees or carry any large limbs. He'd rather go home and lie in his hammock.

Well, Ricky's hard, green tomato reached Anthony just as he turned around to mock us for going into the woods to work. The rock-hard unripe tomato hit him right in the crotch. Pain fired behind his eyeballs. He wanted to scream, but had no voice. We saw him fall forward onto the neatly trimmed green lawn. He didn't move. All three of us looked at each other not knowing what had happened. Then, Ricky started to run toward his brother. I passed him as I sprinted by, and got to Anthony first.

What happened? I asked.

There was no reply. Ricky got there, and demanded to know what was the problem. Was he joking? Was he faking? "What's the idea?" he worryingly demanded of his brother.

Anthony started to moan. He roiled slightly to his side, and held his crotch as he pulled his knees up toward his stomach. There was no color in his face.

"Did you throw a rock?" he cried to his brother with little tear pearls dropping from beneath his eyes.

"No, a green tomato," Ricky answered.

Had Ricky thrown a red tomato, it wouldn't have gone as far, and if it did, it would have simply splattered on impact. The green one was as hard as the end of a baseball bat. The throw was remarkable; almost fifty yards, and the odds of landing exactly where it hit him were a thousand to one. Maybe a million to one. It was a throw from center field right to home plate. I don't think anyone on the Philadelphia Athletics could have made that throw. Even decades later, whenever I'd watch a ball game, and see a throw from the outfield to home plate, I'd recall the greatest arm I'd ever seen. Time neither distorted, nor made it fade away. It was etched into my memory, one great timeless throw. It made no difference that it was a tomato and not a baseball. It's not in any record book, but it was right on target. The perfect throw.

We all sat down on the grass around him watching the agony in his face. It was the first time any of us had witnessed a groin shot. We would all recall Anthony's look, a look like he was near death, and when, in the future, each of us got hit in the groin during a sporting event, or from a bicycle fall, we'd see Anthony's face in the back of our minds.

Luckily, after quite some time, Anthony slowly stood up and could walk home. Yes, he did spend the next few hours just lying in his hammock. We all knew better than to ever throw rocks at anyone. Snowballs were acceptable, but sometimes they too could be dangerous, and now we'd learned that green tomatoes were also off the list of things we could use during our summer battles. We, like Anthony, soon forgot how painful an experience it had been, because Time mostly scared you, and then cheated you of accurate reflections. He will however, on rare occasions, be quite helpful by adjusting your memory to forget things, or at least help dissipate thoughts about some of the pains that we all encounter.

Ricky really felt bad. For a few seconds he thought he'd killed his brother. He just couldn't help Billy and me with the forestry tepee project. He left. We headed into the woods.

"Boy, that was some throw," I said as Billy carried an ax, and I carried a hatchet.

"Sure was," he answered.

"Fifty yards, at least."

"And right on target," Billy concluded.

"What are the odds?" I pondered.

"Yea, what are the odds," he repeated.

When we got into the clearing, the last breath of air stopped moving. We stood and listened to the emptiness of the mostly oak glen. We spotted a few perfect sized dead trees, and a number of smaller sassafras trees among the larger black and white oaks. There had to be a least a dozen other species waiting just for us. Only the oaks were fully-grown, towering over all the other trees. None but the smaller young ones would make ideal eight-foot long poles for our tepee, but maybe they could be used for a guard-fence around our clearing.

We quickly put up the first three wooden poles that we found lying on the ground. One was smooth all the way down its sides; we had to cut away a few old dead limbs off the other two. We tied the three small dead trees together at the top with some old clothesline that we had left there when we first started clearing our new summer fortress on the same day we selected that spot. Now, it would be easy to fill in both dead and freshly cut poles all around the three triangular sides. With each new tiny tree that we added, the stronger and more stable our hut became.

"Hey, Johnny," Billy shouted. "If we put enough trunks on, enough so we can't see through any spaces, I bet it will even keep the rain out."

"It'll take some time to do all that," I replied.

"We'll get more help tomorrow."

"Yea. More help." I repeated.

Billy thought for sure that Tudor, or Ricky would want to join in, but neither of us had learned as yet that every person creates their own motivation, their own desire for experiment, to learn, and to grow. Many times I had to spend a lot of time talking Billy into joining my adventures, so I knew this project would take weeks. Little did I know it would all be over in just a few minutes.

"Come on, Billy said. "Let's cut that dead one we saw when we first walked in."

He headed toward a limbless, eight or nine-foot dead white oak that looked like squirrels had scratched off most of its bark while I looked for the hatchet to join him. It was tall, straight, and thin. It would be easy to carry because it had already dried out. Small trees like this dead one were perfect for our project. They were always harder to cut down because they had dried out and hardened so it would take many more swings of the ax.

He was busy chopping at the base of this old long-dead oak tree before I even got half way there. He never looked up. He never saw the swarm of wasps that he was vibrating out of their nest inside the dead tree. They came out of a hole near the top of the eight-foot tree like Navy fighter jets taking off from a carrier. As I shouted to run, he felt the first sting, then he looked up, and saw what we thought were a thousand angry bees and each of them ready to punish the culprit who had attacked their home.

I sprinted out of the woods, and back into the tomato field. As more bees quickly approached, I dropped the hatchet, and started to outrun them. I was always a fast runner for as long as I could remember. I'd even become a hundred-yard dash man when I got to high school. Billy, on the other hand, was heavier and slower. He carried the ax all the way to the edge of the woods when he felt a second sting. He screamed and ran toward me out into the field. I shouted for him to drop the ax and keep running. He ran as best he could, but was always ten or more yards behind me making himself the bee's primary target. It was scary to see how far the swarm followed us across the tomato patch. He was stung at least two more times, and he wailed in pain as we approached his back yard. By then, most of the bees gave up and returned toward their home in the woods. They let us know it was their domain and not ours.

His mother, having heard his loud screams, ran into the back yard. I yelled to her that bees had stung him, three or four at lest, but it turned out to be five painful wasps welts. He'd be hurting the rest of the day, and also far into the night.

The bees had ended our fort building. We were afraid to return anywhere near that area until after school had started once again in the fall when Time swept away our freedom from routine, and the opportunity to smell a sunbaked summer forest. He also stole some days that we could never get back. Time's imbecilic brother Luck had run along with me that day, but He simply avoided Billy. One or two wasp stings can really hurt, but five had to feel like torture.

I went back to my own backyard and spent the rest of the day cutting cardboard strips that I planned to attach to my bicycle fenders so that they would just touch the spikes as they sped around making a noise that sounded to young ears like a racecar on a drag strip. Elmer, the only dog I ever had when I was a kid, left the shade of his doghouse and came to watch me work with the cardboard. Elmer was getting old, but he still loved to roam the autumn woods on the first day of rabbit season when my father and I went hunting. Feeding and caring for Elmer was one of my responsibilities and I took it seriously. He was a hound dog who was growing old. It was either his dependence or his love for me that made me care so much about how he felt. He was very loyal, and he waited every day for me to return home after I finished my paper route. Elmer wagged his tail and stared at me as I use the thicker cardboard that came from wine boxes, and not the thin cardboard you find helping to keep a new shirt stay in its folded position. The strips had to be attached to the fender arms that ran to the axel. If you put two or three on each side of the back or front wheels, you could create a really neat sound. The faster you peddled, the louder and quicker the roar. That would be my project for the remainder of the afternoon. I had no idea how long it would take for the five fires burning on the skin of my buddy to be quenched. I just wanted to forget the sound of the screams he made as quickly as possible.

It was getting late in the afternoon by the time I finished. My bike was now an imaginary racecar. After a short ride around the house to test it, I went to deliver my newspapers. Afterwards, I put it in the yard shed, and then I carefully walked past the barn and the coal bins; past the corn shed, and stopped very near to the place where Billy received his final sting. The sun was setting and there was no breeze. Even the clouds were frozen in place; they just didn't move. The air was bee-free. There would be no more aerial attacks around my make believe castle, which was my grandfather's old barnyard.

I was certain that the barn area would be safe for another adventure when I heard my mother call that dinner was ready. It was a signal you could hear from many mothers each summer evening when Milway was a land filled with enchantment, adventure, and possibility. There was also danger lurking there, hidden in places that we'd never expect.

There were dogs and cats all over Milway, but no one kept

animals in their houses. Cats had jobs. They hunted the barns and chicken coops to catch mice or rats. A few dogs were just watchdogs, signaling with their barks when strangers came into your yard, but most of the Milway dogs were rabbit hounds or bird dogs. My Elmer was a hound dog. When I was only ten years old, he was a wiz at chasing rabbits. He was free to roam free around our yard and farm area, and he lived in a doghouse at the back of our yard. It was my responsibility to provide water and feed him. We were buddies. Elmer was always so disappointed when I forced him to stay behind when I had to bicycle off to deliver the afternoon newspapers. That was another activity that taught responsibility. Even much later on, when Elmer got very sick, I was taught a mature responsibility.

Milway was filled with real-life classrooms and just about everything was a learning experience as long as you stayed alert and were willing to learn.

3-A

Do you remember the smell of a small town in spring? The postmaster's lilacs and the scent of youth coming out in even the oldest member of the community, old Mr. Kunupka, who at the age of eight-eight still pedals his way about on what is most likely the fist twenty-six inch J.C. Higgins ever made. He does it with the agility of a five-year-old on a tricycle. The subtle scent of the first crocus, and the intertwining aromas of old and new grass all come into a state of paramount importance when the new equinox takes place. It foreshadows the coming summer.

Even through the punishing sound of crumpled automobiles, the old closed-down factory's stale odor, and the iris-burning neon advertisements in the bar windows all distract, Milway, when spring has expanded into summer, and pushed the bleak winter's horizon far away, inspirers a bloom and a brief heightening of old sensations.

Travelers from along the goat paths in Poland, and exiles from the Emerald Island, along with the great-grandchildren of Remus and Romulus have come to plant their seed in a village that is life times away.

Old Popeye (Joe) makes his appearance at dawn and fills his unnecessary pre-breakfast hours doing the valueless deeds that he did in his youth. The pony that he keeps and feeds abundantly, serves no useful purpose in the mid-twentieth century aside from satisfying a little boy's daytime dreams. Possible it acts as the empirical stimulus that old men sometimes need to recall childhood memories from deep cerebral caves. Later in the day, he'd begin his philosophical debates at Squeak's (John's) tavern with Leno or Ed over two-or-three-hour-old stale beer. No one recalls where Popeye's bother, Squeak, got his nickname. Only Time can recall it.

The Mayor usually gets to the Post Office first. Aside from the two taverns in Milway, the Post Office is the focal point of the community. The Mayor is followed by a parade of older and middle-aged men who seek status in the amount of letters they can display ever so haphazardly, while they awaken their well-rested minds to the daily dawn debates.

Patty, Sandra, Gary and little Joey all swing their way to the bus stop with unwanted sweaters drooping over their shoulders, and hats that any ten-year-old could tell you were unnecessarily forced upon their heads by mothers who seem to have forgotten that naked heads and bare arms are proper protocol with which to greet Aphrodite's return.

They busily make senseless conversation while in a maze about the mystic aura hanging in the air this morning. As the children watch for the school bus, and the Mayor and his friends watch them from the porch of the Post Office, Popeye views it all from the bar stool with his comrades of concern, over "eye-openers". Meanwhile, Squeak is busily setting up new bottles with illegible print; the day begins under the auspicious eyes of the new visitor – Spring.

Lilies, lilacs, and lady-slippers have bloomed from beyond my back door, and as Theseus outwitted the fierce Minotaur, so too has Persephone outwitted the hateful Hades. Death, having died, dies no longer, and once again spring returns as proof.

On some mornings, once the buds have bloomed, Old Kunupka coasts in on his bicycle, and like a twentieth-century Aristotle, begins a dialogue of reflections with the more amazed than interested children at the bus stop. He tells them how he learned to read when he was their age, and how he could never get enough of Dickens and of Thackeray. It makes no sense to the children, and they all know that he had never ever been their age.

Within a few days of the new spring, my mother Helen, saw her new lilacs as a source of Cupid's philandery and everybody in town felt sixteen, not remembering how bad it was to be sixteen.

The earth spins and another morning arrives to paint Milway in shades of varied green spectrums, while Popeye presents eulogies for those other morning magistrates who used to dictate meaningful dialogue along with him. They have relinquished that privilege now along with the pains of life in a place beyond where spring comes from.

I never did find out just how many springs Old Kunupka had seen for sure, more than eighty-eight, I'd think. Nor did I ever take time to lament those whom Popeye mentions during his Plato-like presentations of "Things He Knows and Things He Doesn't Know".

Even now, I cannot find stimulation at the break of day with the nectar that Popeye used. I don't ride a bike anymore or stop to play the game of whispering secrets about the past, or of things to come. I don't play kick-the-can anymore.

I avoid the follies of political pragmatisms at any forum like the ones held under the porch at the Post Office. I don't pick Helen's lilacs anymore, lilacs that used to make my mind withdraw into surrealistic dreams of distant caravans like I did when I waited for the school bus, and even earlier when Billy, Ricky, and I walked to school. No, I don't belong to that Milway anymore.

Still, whenever I open a window on a late April's morning with intent to capture the purest of Apollo's golden rays, somehow something I cannot see flies through and optically works on my view of the small town while the scent of blossoms fills my mind with wonder about this tiny hamlet where old men use alcohol at dawn, and lilacs twist the senses while pleas for ever greater liberties sing out on the Post Office porch as Old Kunupka stops to present ancient canticles to children who cannot wait until they too might be where Popeye sits and lectures, or where the Mayor confronts seemingly pertinent political opinions, or simply do as Helen does when she imitates Aphrodite by presenting the world with clusters of lilacs. Time never rests. Time never tires.

I should have left and gone to Philadelphia, Boston, or New York, but Milway, I'm afraid, has been planted deeply within my genes, and my ribonucleic acid is forever telegraphing messages addressed to me saying that I must stay and taste the sights as I drink in the scenes of this tiny village in each new spring, and relive every past summer.

Milway is a small rural town midway between the minor cities of Milltown, over in the next county, and was once a place filled with mills making glass, and the town of Ways Cove where Captain Way landed back in the 1600's after sailing for months from England. Milway is completely different from either of those places, and uniquely different from everyplace else on earth.

4

We grew up with guns. Water pistols, Roy Rogers tin pistols, and real 22 caliber rifles. Most of the men in Milway hunted during the autumn small game season, and during the winter deer season, so in every house there was at least one 12-gauge shotgun large enough to be used for hunting during the December deer season. The 22's were for rats, and other small rodents. They are perfect for teaching marksmanship. Everyone learned to shoot with real ammunition after they were ten years old. Well, all the boys did. Most of us had BB guns, and bows and arrows. We all were taught to be careful and respect each weapon. Even though we didn't know how dangerous it could be, we all helped shoot rats in Ricky's father's chicken coops.

At least twice a year, Spitz, Ricky's uncle, would have Tudor let us all know that there were getting to be too many rats in the chicken coops. With all the chicken feed spread around, each coop would become a rodent heaven. Usually, we'd have only two guys in a room. The average chicken coop was about forty yards long with four, sometimes five, separate rooms in each coop. We'd sneak in quietly, and then very slowly walk the perimeter in opposite directions. Whenever we kicked up a rat, it would make a break for one of the holes along the back walls. We'd have to fire fast. One shot each. We seldom hit them, but the gunfire, even though 22's are quite small, and usually made more of a pop than a bang, echoed much louder inside the coop. We loved the louder sound. We loved the excitement of the hunt. You only had a split second to aim at and try to hit the fleeing rat. I think it was the hunt that scared them away for a while and nothing else. We never reduced their numbers by much, and killed very few of them.

I must have done this for five years or so, starting at ten years old, and only after all those years did I realize that the shells could have easily ricocheted off the concrete blocks and hit one of us. The innocence of youth, actually the stupidity of youth, is what made us feel secure and safe.

My father was an excellent hunter and killed over a hundred and fifty deer in his lifetime. He loved rabbit hunting too, but mostly he was a fisherman. Every time he took me fishing, I loved the smell of the air over the Delaware Bay. Flounders were what we wanted, but many times we came home with a number of other types of fish. We'd clean the scales off them, and remove their insides out in our back yard. It was my job to bury everything we removed from their insides, and also their heads. I'd bury them at the end of our small back yard in a garden where we'd plant lettuce and spring peas every year. The vegetables planted over the fish burial ground always grew best. That was when I learned that nothing should be wasted, and even refuse has a purpose. You always learned far more things during the summer than you ever did during the rest of the year while we were in school. At least it seemed that way when we were twelve. Our summer activities consisted of only one academic course: thinking, which was taught by a tirade of teachers: Time, and his nitwit brother, Luck, and their cousin, Chance, three of the oldest professors in the universe.

Maintenance was the most important thing, my father always said, and he showed me how to wipe off any salt water from the rods, and everything else in our fishing kit. He always had me clean the shotguns after every hunting trip. We hunted every autumn all around the fields near our house, and on the neighbors' properties. We'd walk four or five miles through the woods all the way down to West Boundary Street, the unofficial border of Milway. Even today, whenever I use Hoppe's Power Solvent No. 9 to clean my shotgun barrels, I can recall the aroma of the early morning frosty hunting tours around Milway. It's similar to the recollection I have when I smell cut cedar, and Christmas comes to mind. All the specifics return. The nose is the tunnel entrance into your memory.

Every December my father would take my older brother Jimmy and me down to the cedar swamps off Tuckahoe Road heading toward Dorothy, which was the next town heading south. We went to select, and then cut down our own Christmas trees. They were wild ones growing in hidden spots deep in the cedar swamps. We never bought a spruce or any other kind of tree for Christmas; cedars had a perfect shape, and nothing smelled as good. After my brother could drive, he'd take his buddy Sammy and me down to cut a massive cedar tree just a few days before the holiday. My father had turned that holiday responsibility over to the next generation even though he still enjoyed doing it. Our trees always stayed decorated until January 6th, so there was no rush in putting them up. Today, everything is rushed. People hurry to decorate for Christmas at Thanksgiving diminishing the meaning of Thanksgiving. Some even start right after Halloween. As soon as the holiday gifts are unwrapped, they think about clearing everything out to prepare for the next event. You see Saint Valentine's Day candy in the stores the day after New Year's. Too many grownups have no idea how Time tricks them into letting so many special, unique days, simply fade away.

If the boggy water in the swamp had already frozen, our quest was easy; we'd walk into the swamp on the frozen water. If not, well then, we'd slush through the muddy quagmire until we spotted the ideal cedar tree. It had to form a perfect cone at its top. Once it fell, we'd take off the top six feet to use as our Christmas tree. A tree that smelled as good as it looked. I always felt it was a waste to leave fifteen or twenty feet of cedar alone in the swamp, so many years later after I became an older adult, and when I had to cut the last few trees for my mother's place after my dad died, I made certain to find a six or seven foot field cedar so that there was no waste. Hundreds of them grew along the railroad tracks in Milway, and also all along the wooded edge of all the open fields surrounding the town.

Even today, I put up a real tree; it's always a cedar with its winter holiday aroma, and I never waste any of it. After it's nothing but a ghost of the holiday, it stands against bare oak trees in our yard to give the birds some place to protect themselves from the icy January and February winds. Artificial Christmas trees have no soul, and don't need a period of mourning after their usefulness is ended. A naked Christmas tree, stripped of all its garnishing, and drying out quickly, brittle now, but still green, gave every kid in Milway the opportunity to reflect on how living things fade, and how little concern there is for things or people when they are no longer useful.

I learned decades ago how to spot my ideal Christmas tree during the early part of summer, picture it with lights on it, and then perfect it. Many times I'd trim and manicure the odd limbs a bit so that by late autumn, the six or seven foot field cedar had grown in correcting the empty spots, and filled out into a perfect shape. Time makes it harder for me each year, but I've done it every year since I picked peaches, and helped my mother can them in quart jars so that when the snow was on the ground, and the cedar Christmas tree was decorated, we'd have some of the summer sunshine after dinner for dessert; sunshine that was captured by each peach as it grew into perfection.

Each year it gets harder to recall the words that people said during your youthful years, but you never forget the sounds and smells of your earlier days, especially the magical scents of summer. Many of our summer conversations included the sounds and smells of things that happened well before the sun's heat helped slow our pace, and give us more time for reflections.

The sound of twelve-gauge number six rabbit shot being fired off right after midnight on New Year's Eve is another sound I miss. It's just not done anymore. Once we were old enough to stay up until midnight, my father would head outside, and fire two shots into the night sky. Even Time was forced to stand still for a moment. We'd listen carefully to hear the shots being fired from all over town, and even from far off at homes in the wooded distance. No one knew why they did it. They just did it. I learned many, many years later that it started centuries ago. It was a pagan custom from the early Middle Ages when they wanted to scare off evil spirits from their home areas. Bells rang, pots were banged, and the first gunpowder was exploded. It wasn't like a war, and it certainly was different from the crackling sound of fireworks. It was another magical sound. The echoes of shotgun thunder will never fade from my memory, and it must have been a successful enterprise, because I never saw or encountered any evil spirits. Yes, there were spooky places in Milway; in the cave we would later dig, in the discarded old canning factory, and in many parts of the old barn, but after the New Year's Eve firing of the shotguns, I never even once saw an ominous evil spirit. The tradition continued because it worked.

Hunting rats in chicken coops wasn't the most dangerous thing we did, but at that time in our lives nothing seemed to be dangerous. Youth has no fear, even without knowing that a simpleton named Luck hung around with us nearly every day. I assumed he just wanted to get away from his older brother, Time. We knew wasting the majority of a tree was a sin, and learning the smell of fish guts and chicken intestines never hurt us psychologically. We experienced aspects of living that, for most of us today, have vanished, disappeared, and are not even talked about. I faced danger everyday by today's standards. Just bicycling along the roadways to complete my paper route presented an opportunity for any number of disasters, but that's where we learned to be independent, show personal responsibility, and gain an understanding of everything that life has to offer.

At four o'clock sharp every day except Sunday, an old blue Ford station wagon would pull up and drive into the parking lot of Kupenski Bar's front veranda. Then, it would slow to a full stop, and drop off a bundle of newspapers: the *Vineland Times Journal*, as it was called back then. The newspaper covered the Vineland community over in Cumberland County, and most of the nearby Atlantic County villages. Like Buena Vista Township, of which Milway was a small part. Buena was bigger back then, bigger than the forty-four square mile municipality it is today. It once included all of Landisville and a town called Minotola where the Junior High School was located.

I would unpack the bundle of newspapers, and then I would have to fold each paper in thirds, pack them together into the front basket on my bike, and get them to each house before anyone arrived home from work. The paper was what they all settled down to, usually with a beer. I always checked the baseball standings to see how far the A's, a team now in Kansas City, or the Phillies were behind from first place. I'd been on a Safety Patrol school trip to see the A's play their last year in Philadelphia. The A's finished in 8th place that year, and after that I began to favor and follow the Phillies. The Yankees were always above the A's in the American League, and the Senators were usually tied or just above the Phillies. Then, I'd read all the Headlines.

Headlines tell you everything. Today's modern TV news shows are nothing more than basic headlines.

After speed-reading all the Headlines, I would slowly read the Cut-lines, the captions under all the photos. That quick review usually told me all I needed to know. I saved the funnies for last, and only after I'd completed my perilous tour around mud puddles, potholes, unchained dogs, and on really hot windless days, the swarms of mosquitoes. Mosquitoes swarm at dusk, and that's exactly when I always delivered my papers. The funnies page was my personal reward for another job well done. Being a paperboy was not easy. You never got a day off, well except Sunday, but every other day of the year, hot or cold, wet or dry, I was obligated to get every paper to every house that had ordered one.

After all the papers were folded and ready to fling into the yards, I biked to the first house on my list; it was right next door to the bar where I picked up and folded the papers. There, I would drop off Mr. Joast's paper. He always got the first newspaper. Every single day, six days a week, I hoped that their dog was chained. It usually was, but the little monster would always spring from below the side steps, and take off after me intently gazing at my sneaks on the pedals. Maybe the circular motion of my pedaling incited his anger. I knew he'd sink his teeth into my sneaks if he could catch me before I reached a safe distance. Ironically, he was kept, thank God, on a runner chain, and as soon as he reached the end of it, his head would snap back, and he'd fling around backwards, and lie quietly still on the ground. It took more than a few seconds for him to slowly roll over and then stand up, shake his entire body, maybe to see if everything still worked, and then stagger back to the steps along side of the house. I never got tired of seeing that happen. The dog never seemed to learn that his freedom had an end line, a preset limitation, and I never felt sorry for the stupidity of it all. I knew everyday that it would be a twenty-yard sprint to safety just past the end of his chained restriction. Feeling very pleased that Cerberus, the hound of Hades, hadn't mauled me, I'd continue on with my daily odyssey.

I'd make a right turn, slow down a little, and then head down Cumberland Avenue, which was perpendicular to Tuckahoe Road. Some years after I was away at college they changed the road's name to Broad Street. I called it Cumberland Avenue for at least another decade before I got used to it being Broad Street. That's what it was called in Milltown where it ended. I pedaled west past High Street, the road that Milway School was on, and then I would fly into Tony Mattzeo's yard, toss a paper, then sprint across to Bam's place, another cousin of the De Ross family, all on the right side of Broad Street. Everyday was the same, identical route. I biked west until I got to the county line, which was at Sam De Ross's house. I'd shoot down his driveway, fling the paper onto his front step, and then after a hard U-turn, I'd pick up speed leaving papers at Leo Penerotti's and Romantini's before making another hard right turn onto High Street for John Minlain's, and finally, Tinbucca's. They were right next to each other so I got quickly back onto Cumberland Avenue. From there, the roadway ran downhill for a just over a hundred yards, so I could rest from pedaling, and coast a while. While coasting, I'd lift both legs off the pedals and point them straightforward with one on each side of the front tire. If I kept my feet on the pedals, I would remove both hands from the handlebars and see how far I could coast in a straight line. I usually had to brake a little to slow down enough to be able to put one of the Daily Journals on my Aunt Anna's porch across from the Milway Fire Hall. The last paper on that side of the street went to my second-cousin Carol's house just behind the Milway Hotel.

Carol's father owned and ran the Milway Hotel, but it had seen better days long before I was twelve years old. No more strangers stopped to spend the night. The three-story building stood mysteriously empty except for the first floor bar. It had nothing else to attract customers during the summer that I was twelve and I always felt that Chance's older sister Sorrow must have used some of the upstairs rooms as Her resting place. Chance's baby sister Joy would never have entered the old abandoned rooms.

At the intersection, I'd turn right heading south down Tuckahoe Road where I had to slow down a little because I had to grab two papers for the next location. I pedaled with my left hand on the handlebar, and used my right hand to procure both papers, and quickly get set to let them fly as though the pair were a single thicker volume. Both papers were left at Malatina's. Sonny Penerotti, Leo's brother, lived right behind Malatina's grocery store, so each day he had to walk around the store to the front porch to get his paper. Both papers were always kept out of the rain or snow because I rode right up, and flung them both onto the covered porch. I was certain that they landed in the exact same spot every day. Sonny got his paper and usually took Mrs. Malatina's paper inside for her.

Besides doing the paper route, I also worked part-time for Sonny. Everyone called him Sonny, even the kids in town. I picked eggs in his single hundred-yard-long chicken coop. It was always exciting because you'd have to scare the hens off their eggs, praying they didn't attack your face, and then collect the usually still warm two or three eggs, place them gently in a basket made of wire, and then move on to the next roost and repeat the procedure all over again. During the heat of the summer, the chicken manure was stifling, almost unbearable. In winter it got wet and it was rancid. There are other smells besides a Thanksgiving pumpkin pie that you'll never forget.

The most dangerous part for me came not from the chickens; it was placing the baskets of eggs, one basket at a time, into an egg washer to clean any blood or chicken feces off them. Sonny wasn't known for being extra careful, well, not careful at all, and there was a bare electric wire running from the ceiling light bulb down to the egg washer. Every time I started the machine, I saw sparks, and I knew that it would sooner or later kill me because I never knew for sure if the machine was really off when I had to reach down into the water, and remove the basket of freshly washed eggs. This was far more dangerous than shooting 22 rifles in the enclosed chicken coop buildings over at Ricky's.

Anyway, I always really liked Sonny and his wife. A few years later, when I had to leave Milway School, and attend the district's central Junior High School over in Minotola, Sonny was my bus driver. Both he and his wife treated me like a grownup, and the money I made there I kept, unlike my paper route money that my mother kept. I always found or made whatever I wanted, so I didn't ever really need anything, and it was fine with me that my mother took care of my tiny newspaper salary. Besides, whenever she bought me something that I really wanted like a new baseball glove, or a balsawood airplane kit, she'd remind me that she was paying for it with the money I had made from the paper route. Looking back I know it was a form of positive reinforcement, a way to teach me that you get what you work for.

The newspaper route then took me across the railroad tracks, past my house to Strusser's where I'd ride right around their circular driveway, and toss the paper on their back step. I can't ever recall seeing Billy outside when I was delivering his family's paper. Strange.

Then, I'd leave one at the Spitz's Texaco's station, before driving up a long, long driveway alongside the chicken coops to Ricky's house. It was the last stop for me, and their black beast of a dog was always free and waiting. Unlike the dog at Joast's house, this devil was never on a chain. As I look back I've come to see that the dog had a ritual too; he never charged or attacked me as I rode in. By some strange reasoning, the animal knew he shouldn't prevent me from delivering something to his owners. It was only after I threw the newspaper toward their main door, and circled to start my exit, did the dog spring into action. One slip on the pedal or being just a little too tired, and I knew he'd catch my foot. I'd had dogs bite me, at least two or three times. Not viciously, but enough to draw blood, and I didn't like it. Even today, I am leery of meeting new dogs. As an adult, I now get along quite well with most dogs and every child.

It seemed that no matter how fast I peddled, the dog was always just a bike-length behind me all the way out to the road and therefore, the end of his property line. Either he tired during that sprint, or he knew his family's property limitations, but in either case I was safe once I reached my Grandfather's adjacent land. Only once, the first week I covered this route as a paperboy, did that dog every get to grab my leg. He tore my pants just a bit, but never really hurt me. I'm sure the dog thought of it as a game. I didn't.

I thought of scaring him by throwing some water at him, but I missed him completely when I threw what water was left after half the pint jar splashed out from all the bouncing as I peddled into the yard. Holding the pint jar with my right hand, and the handle bar with only my left hand was not as easy as I thought it would be on a rough gravel driveway. On the tarred street, I could pedal with no hands on either handlebar. During that summer, I learned that few things in life are as easy as you think they are going to be.

When I was with Ricky, down in their wine cellar or playing in their coops, the dog never bothered me. It had to be the spokes of the wheels, and not me personally that irritated the dog. Even today when I irritate someone, it's never done maliciously. I look for some mystic outside source that caused the irascibility. I never notice nor am aware of any personal irritating action as the cause of the problem.

*   *   *

I did a lot of bicycling. Every boy in town was free to ride anywhere, as long as we were back by dinnertime. We learned personal responsibility.

Easter was on Sunday April 1 that year, and it had already been warm. None of us could do much of anything on Good Friday. It was supposed to be a quiet, sad day, but on Holy Saturday, I gathered the full gang and we went off together to play. Ricky,

Anthony, Billy, and I had been hiding some left over firecrackers from the previous Fourth of July. Like money in a spendthrift's jacket, they were burning a hole in our pockets. We all rode across the tracks, south on Tuckahoe, and then west on McDonald Avenue to the old, now-closed landfill and gravel pit that started at Line Street. McDonald Avenue was still just a gravel road, and it was harder to peddle your bike than on the regular tar and cinder roads. It would be quite a few decades before any Milway road was smoothly asphalted.

At the gravel pit, the hills of orange gravel were inviting, and our imaginations swept us into a battle scene somewhere against the Japanese. We all ran up and down the hills carrying sticks and making machine gun noises. A few minutes later, Ricky found an eighteen-inch piece of rusted pipe. I lit one of the firecrackers and threw it like a hand grenade to the top of one of the gravel mounds. The noise excited us, but it was the smell of the exploding power that I remember most.

Ricky and Billy started to set up the pipe as a mortar. We'd drop a lit firecracker down the pipe, and then quickly shove a stick in after it to see if the stick would fire out toward the enemy.

"Try just a cracker, first," Anthony suggested. "No mortar."

"Good idea," I said.

Look at this old broom handle. It's just perfect for the mortar. It just fits inside the pipe," Ricky said.

I struck another match slowly, lit the firecracker Billy was holding, and Billy shouted, "Bombs away!" as he dropped the explosive down the pipe.

One, two, three seconds seemed like forever before the firecracker went off. Boom! It scared Anthony enough to make him let go of the pipe as a puff of gray smoke rose from the pipe.

"Okay," Anthony said after he saw there wasn't any real danger. He was ready for the mortar shot. He got on his knees and held the pipe between them as he slanted the make-believe mortar toward the woods line past the last gravel mound. "Johnny, let Billy light it, and you drop it down. Ricky will insert the broom-handle. That'll be our mortar. It should blow it right out. Use the Cherry Bomb, not those little Mary Jane's."

"I'm ready," I said.

"Me too, " Billy said.

"So am I," Ricky concluded.

Strike. Lit. Dropped, Insertion. We all jumped back as the explosion occurred. No broom-handle mortar flew up. Stones, however from the bottom flew back toward Anthony like dozens of cannons, all being fired at once. It threw the shrapnel at him. One jagged stone cut right through his jeans. Together, they created three welts on each leg. The one that hit him directly on the left knee, make him screech with pain. He limped back to the bikes, and could barely pedal back home. The war was over. There was one pack of Mary Jane's, and five Cherry Bombs that we wouldn't use until the Fourth of July, and then, for sure, there would be no mortar.

The gravel pit had some ponds of water in it that froze over every winter. They were barely okay to walk and slide on, but not very good at all for ice-skating. These frozen small ponds were not big enough for a real hockey match, but during the blistering days of summer, the gravel pit was a gigantic sandbox filled with orange gravel where those of us who were soldier-ready could play, and fight battles to keep the world safe, and provide freedom for us all. Not the freedom of a democracy, but the freedom of absolute youth.

5

My brother Jimmy asked me to come hold a ladder while he put up a basket rim against the outside of the old barn's eastern wall. It had no windows on that side, was made of clapboard wood, and had enough space between the back wall and the scale house for a half-court game. Out of bounds was standing on the truck scale at the start of the coal bins. He suggested that I sweep the dirt to get rid of as many stones as possible; otherwise, it would be much harder to dribble the ball. Milway had its first basketball court. It was outside with a hard-packed dirt surface, but it was the best we could do. Besides, it was perfect for playing "Out" or any game where you had to repeat your opponent's type of successful shot.

Jimmy always had me do things he didn't want to do. That's why he told me to sweep the stones off the playing area. He was seven years older than me, and would soon graduate high school. Then, he'd quickly join the Navy. He wanted to leave Milway as soon as possible, while I wanted to stay there forever. Our house, and all of Milway would be entirely mine as I grew older, and let Time sneer at the both of us even if we were in different places. Time can do that. Distance means nothing to Him. You may think He's different in far away places, but He's exactly the same. It's we who are different as the distance between us grows further and further away. Jimmy wanted to be older. I was certain that I'd be twelve forever.

Our new Basketball Court had a real basketball rim, exactly ten feet high, and imaginary lines on the court. The rim, however, had no net. I thought my Grandfather would rip it down so that we wouldn't damage the barn's exterior wall, but when he'd peeked across the street from his front porch swing when we were all playing Boston Celtics against the Philadelphia Warriors, he said nothing. Few people remember the Syracuse Nationals becoming the Philadelphia 76ers, but that was after Time and Luck changed us forever.

Since the court was very close to my house, and we had the only basketball for most of that summer, I was able to practice dribbling and shooting layups every afternoon when the heat from the sun's furnace faded, and its rays of fire sank below the roof line of the barn. The apex of the barn would then leave the court in its cooling shadow. I was always a fast runner, but had to learn to dribble the ball while running. When the ball hit some of the exposed stones, you had to quickly regain control of it and keep dribbling. Rebounding was a different skill. The taller kids could easily get more rebounds without even jumping. After a while, they seemed to forget how to jump. I learned how to sneak in front of them and then jump for the ball, and I learned to run and dribble the ball faster than anyone else. I quickly acquired the skills necessary to dribble the ball without looking at it. I took advantage of using our court every chance I got.

Practicing those skills would really pay off when I got to Cleary Junior High School where, even though I was far from being the tallest player, I could handle the ball better than anyone, and almost never missed a layup. Stones. It was the stones. When you dribble a ball on a hard, packed gravelly soil, and it hits a lot of small stones all the time, you have to acquire the skill to keep control of it. I did. I could dribble a basketball with perfect control even when bigger opponents swiped at it. My coach said I'd never be a Warrior, but I was his starting point-guard. I loved playing sports far more than classroom studies. However, since I always saw my father reading, books didn't scare me. Reading wasn't as much fun as running barefoot through the wet green grass filled with the morning dew, bicycling all the back dirt roads of Milway, or even helping pick, skin, and put-up peaches for the winter, but it slowly grew on me. I figured I could do all those summer things and read too. From that summer on, I read something every night before I fell asleep. That season prepared me for Junior High School, and also for every other year in my life that came after the summer I was twelve.

I had a twenty-four inch J.C. Higgins bike from the Sears store in Vineland. Jimmy's bicycle was a bigger twenty-six inch bike, and he made me ride on his handle-bars instead of letting me ride mine along side him during the few times he wanted to be bothered with his pain-in-the-neck little brother. We rode over to Sammy's where the two big guys talked about cars. Ricky and I walked down to the gas station, and shared a Coke with his cousin Tudor who had to watch the station after school, and even during a number of weekdays during the summer. In the office at the gas station there was the greatest pinball machine in the world. I suppose it was for the children of people waiting to get their oil changed. I never saw anyone using it except us.

You were supposed to put nickels in to play, but that summer the glass cover got loose. We never knew who took the screws out, Tudor maybe, because he had to spend so much time there, but we found all you had to do was slide back the glass cover, and put your little finger into the slot that recorded the number of games you had won. Normally, you paid and played. If you did well, and scored a lot of points, the machine rewarded you with a free game, sometimes two.

We'd trigger the mechanism with our little fingers, and the pinball machine would register four or five games as available for free. I seldom ever had an extra nickel, but I played the pinball machine at least twice a week during the greatest summer any kid could ever have. It was one of the earliest types of hand-eye coordination activity machines. Modern video games couldn't ever compare to the sights and sounds of a pinball machine.

"Johnny," I heard my brother's voice echo.

I left the machine right in the middle of a game fearing my brother would be mad.

"Let's go, Johnny," I heard Jimmy call me again as he neared the gas station entrance on his bike.

"Here I am," I answered.

I ran out and hopped up on the handlebars. I placed one hand on each side of me straight down on the handlebars. Then I put my left foot on the front fender, and my right foot on top of my left one. I had to put one foot on top of the other to stay balanced. Jimmy took off like a rocket with me shouting to slow down all the way back to our house.

He said nothing. His silence scared me more than the excessive speed. I know he'd think it funny if I fell or flew off when he stopped. All of the older kids in town seemed to have a much different sense of humor than any one in my younger gang did.

We flew past the barn and turned into our driveway heading toward the red garage between my house and the barn. It was two cars wide, but had bays deep enough for two vehicles to be parked in each side. In the rear on the left side was the pit. My uncles and father used it to change oil in their own cars, tractors, and coal trucks. Anytime your muffler got a hole in it, you'd pulled in over the pit, which was about three feet wide and eight feet long, and deep enough to stand up in while replacing an oil filter or wrapping asbestos insulation around the hole in your muffler. It was a multi-purpose pit. We used asbestos materials all the time, and had no idea what the future would have to say about it.

"Slow down!" I shouted. "Slow down!"

He silently flew toward the garage.

"Stop, stop!" I screamed.

Still saying nothing, Jimmy headed toward the open pit side of the garage, and finally slammed back on the pedals to brake.

Inertia should have thrown me forward to the ground, and possibly into the pit. I held on to the handlebars for dear life. Jimmy would have thought it really funny if I flew off and into the pit. The bike stopped. I fell to the ground, rolled over right at the edge of the pit, jumped up, and ran away as fast as I could, as I heard him shouting, "I wouldn't let you fly into the pit." Maybe he really had my safety well calculated, but in my mind, dumb old Luck was also on the bike, and He had just cut me a break. Whenever Luck does you a favor, there's no way to repay Him.

I knew he meant just the opposite of what he had shouted to me. We didn't become real friends until decades later after my mother passed away. But for the rest of that summer, and until he left home after finishing high school, I never rode on his handlebars again. I was no genius, but I wasn't stupid either. I learned to avoid situations that might kill me. The only way to repay Luck for all the favors He did for me was to learn how to avoid situations that would result in getting some injury or even worse. I didn't know much about death at that age, but I was sure Time and His irrational brother, Luck, knew about it. Before summer was over, Jimmy would unknowingly teach me all I'd ever need to know about it.

The outdoor basketball court, the pinball machine, and insane bike rides couldn't compare to the firecrackers, tomato fights, or swarms of wasps, but summer lingered on slowly, and I just felt, maybe sensed, that there was something better I could be doing.

*   *   *

The freedom our parents gave us was remarkable. Personal responsibility was taught to every child, and every child accepted that responsibility. We bicycled further than we were permitted. We climbed trees and buildings we were told to avoid. We took a lot of calculated chances and survived.

After the bicycle ride on my brother's handlebars, I went to deliver my newspapers. I noticed the bike didn't sound the same. The next morning, I saw that the arm-brace that ties my back fender to the axil had come loose, and had to be bolted back on. We had hundreds of odd sized bolts and nuts in the barn shop, and I quickly found a bolt to replace the lost one. I couldn't fine a washer that fit, so I slowly and carefully rode across the tracks to Angelo's gas station. We had two gas stations in town, but Angelo's was more of a car maintenance center with auto parts and old cars everywhere. Spitz just pumped gas and changed the oil.

"What ya looking for?" Angelo asked, as I rode up. He was sitting in the old metal chair in front of the building where he could be seen every single day. Both he and the chair looked a hundred years old to me.

"I need a washer for this nut to hold my fender onto the back axle."

"Got thousands of them…if you can find them," he said. "Try the back bench first. That size might be there."

Angelo treated all of us like family. I went into the garage and started to search, checking each washer I found against the nut I'd brought along to use as a measure. The place looked like more of a junkyard than an active auto garage. I spent over ten minutes before finding one that would fit.

"Can I have this?" I asked.

Angelo never answered. He turned my bike upside down, grabbed an adjustable wrench, and took the nut I had. He slipped on the fender support, put on the washer, and then tightened the nut over it. Perfect.

"Anything I can help with?" I asked wanting to repay the favor.

"Sure," he said. "You can replace the brake lining in that Dodge if you got time."

Everyone I grew up with was a flood of subtle sarcasm. They would yell if you broke something, but mostly it was just an avalanche of wisecracks. You had to learn thinking skills, and know how to interpret everything you heard.

"Thanks," I said as I turned the bike over to an upright position. "I don't have time to fix the brakes right now."

I got seated on the bike, and decided to test the fender by riding a few hundred yards south on Tuckahoe Road down toward the old canning factory. It had been vacated for years. It held mystery. Lingering in its dark corridors, haunting the dark old buildings, was Time, sitting there all by Himself.

*   *   *

The site consisted of two buildings. There was an old wooden office building, filled with discarded papers that were most likely tossed about by my older brother and his friends years ago, long before I and my buddies ever ventured into the place. A few years after the summer of 1956, this old wooden structure would catch fire and burn to the ground. Nothing remained but the block foundation.

The second, and much larger building housed the canning lines with conveyer belts and empty filling tanks. It also had an upstairs section. My mother couldn't even remember when it closed down; sometime during the Great Depression, so whenever we safaried through the place, Time toyed with us. He made us think we were the first explorers to ever be in there. We weren't. There was nothing left to discover among the empty cans, conveyer belts, and half-rotten cardboard containers. However, every sunrise presented a new world for us, and summer was the time for exploration. I figured I'd get the guys, and we'd all come back tomorrow. Then, I would lead the invasion of this wondrous old castle-like structure. There's not only strength in numbers, there's much less fear when you're not alone. That's a rule to follow whenever you decide to visit some spooky old place.

My bike was fixed. My mind was busy with tomorrow's plan. A train was coming, and I could maybe count its cars to a new record. The breeze was blowing from the southwest, where there were more pine trees than oaks, and the air was filled with their unique, particular scent. I was certain I could hear the scent of pine marching toward the center of Milway. Summer had definitely set in because my uncle Mike was mowing the field along side our house with his tractor and brush-hog. He mowed and then plowed this field every year as soon as my mother's lilacs faded away. The aromas of the newly cut wild rye made itself ready to battle with the flow of pine scents approaching from the nearby forest. Everything was as it should be.

Uncle Mike was approaching the wood-line near the end of the field exactly where I kicked up a covey of quail every November during the first week of small game hunting season. That's where we'd rake the dead leaves into a few small piles far enough away from our house to be safe, and then we'd burn them. You could have bonfires back then. Now it's against the law. In second or third grade, Mrs. Sneely had read a story to us about some kid's Uncle Zeke, who did the same thing with the leaves in his yard. All the children in the area came to watch the mesmerizing effect of the flames, and smell the toasty smoke. I had learned quickly that each type of leaf has its own peculiar aroma. I never smoked any cigarettes when I grew up because I found the burning tobacco to be a most offensive odor. Tobacco is one leaf I've never cared for, so I avoided it. After all the leaves that Zeke raked into a pile were burned, which took an hour or more, Zeke brought out forks; one for each kid. He then dug into the ground under the largest pile of burnt leaves. The ground was like an oven door. He would pull sweet potatoes out of the steaming sand, set them on the wooden yard table, slice them open, cut a chunk of butter from the butter sticks he had in his coat pockets, spread each opened potato with golden butter, and then, in complete unison, all the kids dug into the best baked sweet potato they'd ever eat in their lives. I couldn't swear that the burning leaf event was really in a storybook; maybe Mrs. Sneely just make it up.

Real or not, we tried it once, but we only did it one time. We tried to repeat the experience of those fictional kids, and their Uncle Zeke, but our potatoes were not completely cooked, they were a little too hard, and our leaf-burning-potato-baking left a completely different memory in our minds. We tried. We failed. But isn't that how you learn? We never did it again, not because it didn't work so well, but because Milway end-of-the-summers had too many other things to do. Besides, there was never enough time to repeat anything. Only baseball games, Kick-the-Can evenings, and repeated raids into vegetable gardens were ever thought worthy enough to do more than once.

Old man Time set the rules; we didn't. As I look back on this, I realize that life never gets easier than when you were twelve. Luckily, the older you get the faster time flies by, and so does each difficulty you have to endure. The problems and troubles you encounter when you're older seem to last a longer time, but in reality, they last a much smaller percentage of your existence.

5-A

I found out much later on in my life that in 1956 my parents made just about $4,000 a year. My father was looking for a new car, and he found that a new Plymouth would cost just over $2,000. It was the year when gasoline cost twenty-two cents a gallon at both of Milway's gas stations. Spitz caught the people heading toward Ways Cove and Atlantic City, while Angelo served cars heading down to the Jersey shore from the northern communities, and even from Philadelphia.

Between the two gas stations, my grandfather's shop in the barn, or at anybody's yard shed; yes, everyone had a storage shed in their back yard or attached to a garage, you could find anything you'd ever need to fix a bike, build a fort, or defend your play area from Nazis or monsters.

In clear black and white we saw General Eisenhower and Mr. Nixon nominated at the national Republican Convention on television. The Democratic Convention chose Mr. Stevenson and Estes Kefauver, a bizarre name that we all liked to pronounce. Ricky would pronounce it very slowly: "keyyy-fahhh-errr". Elvis was a really different name too, but Elvis Presley's, *Heartbreak Hotel*, was on the radio everyday. It was the first of his 170 hit singles.

Carl Perkins, Johnny Cash, and Jerry Lee Lewis were also names we heard about on the radio. When we heard the songs played on the radio that never stopped broadcasting in the office at Spitz's gas station, we'd make up stories about who was singing them. I once said to Ricky, "I bet none of those guys could ever beat us at Kick-the-Can, or ever had a real tomato fight. You know, one right in a tomato field"

Ricky agreed. So did Billy, Anthony, and Tudor. Agreeing was bonding. You learn to disagree as you grow older. So when you're really old, you just disagree with everybody about everything. It just happens.

We were all wrong about the tomato fight. All three of those singers grew up almost like we did. So it would be a smart bet to say they all threw something, maybe a tomato, at some of their friends, and surely must have kicked something during their own youthful rural summers.

I kept thinking about baking sweet potatoes in the gravelly sand beneath a burning pile of dead leaves, but the only flames we saw in summer were campfire flames. Darting and dancing like Asian dancers; amber and yellow colors intertwining, and the dangerous part of every inferno, of course, made every boy fascinated with fire. I always wondered what the first cavemen thought about when one of their clan members first brought a burning stick into their cave to start a fire of their own? The light from the fire extended the day into the night, pushed back the icy air, and changed how theirs, and everyone else's food, would taste forever more.

We seldom went out anywhere as a family. We did go see a movie called, *The Ten Commandments* in October after the greatest summer in all of history had ended, and we once went to a place called Captain Starn's, right alongside the ocean, in Atlantic City. I almost never went out to eat. Restaurants scared me a little as I recall. I had to wear my only dress-up apparel, a pale blue sports jacket to get into Captain Starn's. People dressed up to go out to eat for the same reason they put flowers on a dining table, to make it a more beautiful experience. I think having to wear my sports jacket, and looking like a grownup made my meal taste much better. I learned much later on that you should use all five senses when you're eating to truly enjoy a civilized meal. Peanut butter and jelly sandwiches don't count. But as for *The Ten Commandments*, I didn't care as much for the story's plot as I did for all the miracles Moses did…with God's help, of course. The movie was in full color, and was shown on an enormous screen, and that made me begin to dislike our black and white television a little. Well, maybe just disappointed with it more than disliking it. After all, I couldn't see *Flash Gordon* anywhere else.

My brother, Jimmy, told me he had to imagine in his head all the scenes taking place during the *Lone Ranger* radio broadcast, and that television would make me stupid. I wondered if any of my older uncles ever told him that radio would make him stupid. Radio gave him all the words and background sounds that a book cannot provide. Radio would limit his imaginational skills. I didn't want to be stupid, but it didn't bother me too much. I told him that *Flash Gordon* showed stuff we could never imagine ourselves because it was all in the future, and nobody could imagine what even tomorrow will be like, let alone in the far, far future. Every tomorrow is just a guess. I'd rather be surprised by each new tomorrow, and wouldn't even try to guess about it. All the wonder in life starts with being surprised. And wonder actually starts and ends with being twelve years old.

My mother spent a half an hour every weekday watching CBS's, *As The World Turns*, on our tiny television screen. I still don't know why. It had nothing at all to do with astronomy.

My father shaved with a Gillette razor, and watched the Gillette *Friday Night Fights* on TV. Before summer began, one late April Saturday afternoon, he told me Rocky Marciano had retired as the undefeated Heavyweight Champion of the World. "Wow!" I told him, "Nobody in the whole world could beat him." My father was the best block-layer in the world, I thought, but that didn't compare at all to being undefeated at something.

Whenever a singer named Little Richard shouted out a song called *Tutti Frutti* from the radio, my mother would quickly change the station. On television, some Egyptian called Nasser pledged that he would take back Palestine, but that was old news. Didn't Moses come from Egypt to do the same thing over three thousand years before Nasser? Somebody named Golda Meir became Israel's foreign minister. Marilyn Monroe married some playwright called Arthur Miller.

Most importantly to us was that a guy named Dumas, Charlie Dumas that is, not the writer Dumas that I'd read years later, was the first guy to ever jump over seven feet in the high jump track event. That's almost over your doorway threshold. Wow! When we played at track and field events, jumping over a horizontal stick resting at four feet high, and then falling onto a pile of sawdust without knocking it off, was, we all thought, worthy of a medal.

I said that the most important news of the entire summer had to be that Dean Martin and Jerry Lewis were breaking up. They did their last show on July 24 at some nightclub in New York City. On July 30, they authorized "In God We Trust" as the US motto. Except for the Martin and Lewis breakup, none of it meant very much to any twelve-year-old anywhere. I'm sure some other things must have happened too, but you can't change the past, so look to the future, but mostly, make today count the way my buddies and I made everyday be extra special during the summer of 1956.

I remember that we had a whole extra day in 1956, but it was a Wednesday, and not an extra Saturday. I thought about some kids having their birthdays on February 29, and only having their birthday parties once every four years. Rotten luck.

We didn't have to go back to school until September 5. Nothing lasts forever. However, during the heat of late June, and into July, we thought that this summer just might go on forever. I could feel when Time was trekking along with us on certain summer days, and even sense when his numbskull brother, Luck, was around us, but their first-cousin, Chance, kept hidden most of the time. She had a younger sister named Joy, who liked nearly all of my buddies, but Chance's older sister, Sorrow, mostly ignored us in the same way that all the older guys in Milway mostly ignored us. She liked to sit in on the conversations of our parents and grandparents. They must have had more in common with her than we did. Chance's two sisters never spent any time together. Sorrow could be cruel if She wanted to be, like when She'd see Joy giggling with us, and having fun, She'd sweep by and remind us about September fifth, and then quickly disappear. It wasn't a topic She usually dealt with, but it could put a dark cloud over our enjoyment and She knew that.

None of us ever wanted it to become September fifth. Wouldn't be it nice, we thought, if Milway were an anomaly in the universe, and Time couldn't exist, occur, or even visit our grapevines, our chicken coops or our barn? How wonderful, I thought, it would be if our farms and fields, our gravel pits and abandoned buildings stayed the same forever. Learning there's no such thing as immortality means you've grown up. It shouldn't have to happen until both sisters, Joy and Sorrow, completely ignore you.

6

The month of June was disappearing quickly, and I checked with Ricky to see if his cousins from Pennsylvania would be visiting him for the Fourth of July. They always brought firecrackers, sparkler's, and once they had a skyrocket that exploded high above Billy's chicken coop, the same coop they'd just begun to tear down. We fired it off from Ricky's yard, but it burst its fire-filled colors high above Billy's yard across the street.

"Yes they would," Ricky answered. "Armand will be sure to bring a few cherry-bombs. I'd bet on it. He always does."

Being secure of what lay ahead for us during the following week, the three of us mounted our bikes, and rode off to the old factory. As usual, Billy rode the slowest. Ricky and I rode ahead hoping no one else was around. We all turned off Tuckahoe Road to hide our bikes in the bushes along side McDonald Avenue just behind the old factory building. There was no need to bring any attention to our breaking and entering. If it were meant to be open for visitors, most of the place would not have been boarded-up. However, it was easy to get in because the plywood door coverings were no longer hanging tightly after so many years of protecting the doorway. Inside, there were long lines of machinery for filling the quart cans of tomato sauce and one machine, we thought, that would put the tops on each can as it sped by filled with Jersey tomato sauce. I was most fascinated with the end of the line where two iron arms still had badly faded labels in them showing a bright red Jersey tomato. Because most of the windows were covered, the place was dark, and to be honest, a little scary. Ricky always thought bums, or railroad hoboes, were hiding in the corners and crevices. The tension created by thinking that heightened our adventure as we explored through this time warp, and journeyed through a place only our grandparents knew when it was active and alive.

We'd been in there a few times before but for the first time we were making our way toward the steps and about to see what the attic, or rather just an upstairs level, had hidden in its long dead space.

"It's brighter up there," Billy noted.

"Yea," I followed. "There's no boards over the upstairs windows."

"Great," Ricky said.

"You ever been up there?" Billy asked.

"Nope," we both replied simultaneously.

"Watch out for broken steps," I said.

"If they never got wet, they'll be okay," Ricky replied as Billy led the way.

When we walked through the upstairs doorway, we saw that the doors had been removed, maybe stolen, a long time ago. The frames were filled with dust, and the hinges were totally rusted. The long rectangular room had a high celling and would have made a great basketball arena, except for the fact that the floor had too many rotten spots. Water leaks had made our trek precarious. Take a wrong step and your leg might just go through the floor. There were some cardboard boxes, lots of browned and torn tomato sauce labels, but not much more scattered about over most of the floor. We all thought our expedition was a failure, that we hadn't found anything new, until we spotted a stack of glass cubes piled neatly below the middle window of the empty hall.

"I know what they are," I told them. "They're glass blocks. My father is a mason, and he had worked with them once in Somers Point. They filled in a large window space with them."

"Neat," Ricky said. "You have a solid wall, but light can still get through."

"Yea," Billy added. "That's neat."

"My father said there's a vacuum or air space in the center of each one so they insulate as good or better than a wooden wall," I added.

A masonry cinder block was sixteen inches long. These were eight inches high, like the blocks were, but only eight inches long. These glass blocks were just four inches wide, half a regular eight-inch cinder block. You'd need two for every half block. They were heavy, made with really thick glass. It looked like there was just air in an empty space in the center. I never paid any attention to that whenever I had walked pass a place that used them along side their entrances in place of a window. But the deep centers of each block caught, and held our attention. There was nothing there. If it was a vacuum, well okay, but if it held some air captured on the day it was made, well then, if we broke one open, we'd be releasing something from the past into our present. It was too much to think about.

"Let's drop one out the window," Ricky suggested.

The backside of the building was completely empty. There was a broken sidewalk running along the back section of the building we were in. There was nothing else but overgrown vines, and new trees filling in what may have once been a parking lot long before I was born. At least it's not a cat, I thought to myself. We're almost three stories up; higher than Tudor's back steps.

The window, we assumed, would push out easily, but to accomplish our destructive act, we'd need to go back down stairs, find a chair or table, and have something to stand on to reach the window, and be able to see the result of dropping the glass block from more than two and a half stories up. It would be easy to hit any of the large sections of the old concrete sidewalk. We wanted to watch it make its journey all the way down to the broken sidewalk, and see it shatter.

Billy and I went downstairs, quickly found two very old chairs, and took them both upstairs. All three of us could stand on the two chairs with the middle guy straddling both chairs. We pushed the window open and were happily surprised by how easily it moved. Ricky jumped down, selected a glass block to sacrifice, handed it to me, and asked me to wait until he was back up and could watch the first bombing run.

I held out my arms as far as I could reach.

Billy shouted, "Let her go!"

I opened my fingers just enough to feel the glass cube slide away from me just as yesterday had slid out of our hands and away from us all.

Boom! It exploded like an artillery shot when it hit the sidewalk. Glass fragments flew everywhere, and we were glad we were high above it, and not standing anywhere nearby the impact area.

"Oh my God!" exclaimed Ricky. "I never thought it'd make so much noise! Wow. It's a bomb!"

"It must be the vacuum in the middle," I said.

"Do you think they heard it at Angelo's garage?" "Might have," Billy answered Ricky's question. Without worrying about who might have heard it, he continued, "That was really cool."

I said, "Let's wait a while, and see if anybody comes before we test another."

"Good idea," said Ricky.

While waiting, we all went downstairs and found a semi-stable folding table. We took it upstairs, and lifted four more glass blocks onto it alongside the window. That brief summer afternoon was both scary and exhilarating. It beat building forest forts, winter's ice hockey, shooting rats in chicken coops, and was far better than baseball or basketball. We were our own Air Force, dropping bombs on a make believe evil enemy that was trying to destroy everyone's freedom; trying to invade the walls around our ancient village.

We waited until the crickets began to chirp again; birds in the nearby woods sang just as they were doing before our first experiment, and until there was no sound of any nearby car or truck. If the first drop was on Hiroshima, our second drop would target Nagasaki.

Boooom! The second glass block hit the exact same place on the broken sidewalk below our window. This time most of the glass attacked the sidewall of the building, and didn't fly much elsewhere. It was safer for anything crawling around in the weeds below. The angle at which it hits, must determine the direction that the glass shrapnel blast out, we concluded.

We were even more impressed with the second bomb than the first. We dropped another two, one to the right, and one to the left of the original site. The excitement was waning after that, so our fifth and final bombing attack against the defenseless sidewalk seemed anticlimactic. Boooom! The fifth exploded just like all the others did, but it seems that young minds have very short attention spans. Even massive explosions cannot hold a young boy's attention for very long. A twelve-year-old brain continuously needs new input. It has so much space to fill.

We closed the window and left. By the time we got to our bikes, nature's noises had once again returned, and the full heat of the summer sun roasting us on the windless day began to create thoughts of cooler places. A swim down at Kimble Bridge on the way to Milltown; running through some garden sprinklers, or maybe just a fight with water balloons might ease the torture of the sun. We didn't usually feel the heat the way that grownups often do, but maybe, just maybe, our nerve endings were still firing from the excitement of the glass-block bombing raid we'd just experienced.

*   *   *

The extra heat created from having to pedal our bikes so much was partly neutralized by the air we moved through, so we kept riding. By the firehouse was a tiny stream, really an old drainage ditch dug out by the WPA Depression work programs. The draining swamp water in it was actually the very headwaters of the Tuckahoe River that we crossed over whenever we went to the seashore. We left our bikes by the steps of the Protestant Church, and walked the remaining thirty yards to the little creek, where we took off our sneaks and stood in the slowly running water. All three of us cupped up a handful and drank it. With today's farm fertilizer run off, litter, and who knows what else, it would probably kill you, but Time didn't have any of us scheduled for that yet.

The stream was at the start of a large wooden block of swampy trees. During the school year, we'd all hike into that piece of woods every weekend, and just before summer vacation started, we built a small encampment not far in from the road. On some schools days, we'd go early, stop by the fort to check it out, and then rush off to school in time to help raise the flag. It was always an honor to be selected to raise the flag on the flagpole just outside the school building at the front entrance.

Since there was always some water lying in the swampy pools around the fallen trees all over the boggy lot, we had to walk along logs, jump over two larger fallen trees, and only then could we enter the base we'd built. It was near the end of May, of that same year, just before school was let out for our summer of '56, when Tudor joined Ricky, Billy, and me, as we went into the wet woods before school was ready to start. We all got to the fort safely walking along logs, jumping over puddles, and then each person made a suggestion as to what else was needed to complete the mini Alamo.

"Okay. Saturday. We'll all meet right here," I said. "Right after breakfast."

"Time to go," said Billy. "The bell gonna ring soon."

"I think it's my turn to put up the flag," Ricky said. "I can't be late."

Splat! The sound of a giant fly swatter hit our ears simultaneously. We all turned backwards toward Tudor who was behind our procession that was heading out to the road. He'd slipped off the largest log we had to walk along, and fell backwards onto the spongy moss growing in about two inches of water. He jumped up like nothing had happened, and continued journeying out to the road, and then he scurried off to school with the rest of us. His entire back was wet, and so was his rear end. By pure luck, no water had gotten into his shoes.

I'd probably have gone home and changed, but Tudor, for some unknown reason, was afraid to be late. When we arrived at school, Tudor kept his face toward the teacher at all times. He went to the boy's lavatory, wrang out his shirt, squeezed out the rear end of his pants, and returned to the classroom. He was a grade ahead of me, so he sat in a different row in the multi-class room in the Milway schoolhouse. His row was doing numbers. Long division, I think. We were trying to fill in the names of the states on a blank map. I hoped to get at least forty correct of the forty-eight blank spots shown.

At recess, Tudor told us that he had mostly dried out, everything that is, except his underwear. We never worried about being dirty or wet during summer, but to have to sit still, all day, in the cool May weather, not in the tropical heat of summer, had to be as torturous as the 1942 Bataan Death March in the Philippines we'd heard about. I think he was simply embarrassed, and tried not to make a big deal about it, so we too ignored what happened, and just let him dry out.

He did not show up the following Saturday when we met to finish the job. Three of us completed what we had to do, but we never returned to it anymore until late August when the entire area had dried up, and performing the careful balancing act on the logs and limbs was not needed to reach the fort. It's always easier when things are out of sight if you want to keep them out of your mind.

Tudor never visited that fort again; Ricky too, came less and less. Only Billy and I would venture into that location during the late summer weeks. Every time we went there, we talked about the day Tudor fell off the fallen tree, and got so wet. We figured that you never really know what you'll have to put up with until the time comes when it happens to you. I figured that we'd all get tested sooner or later because Chance is always presenting options for you to try.

None of our group was selected to raise the flag that day. Ricky had miscalculated just as Tudor had done. It seems that Time was never concerned if we were late or punctual. His imprudent brother, Luck, confirmed that He could pinpoint His attention very carefully, and He targeted just Billy, Ricky, and me that early morning on our way to school. For some unknown reason, goofy Luck, just ignored Tudor.

7

Helping my Uncle Mike fill, weigh, and then deliver furnace coal during the icy months was always an adventure, but we didn't do it during summer. We seldom, if ever, started to deliver coal before October's chilly breath was felt. Watching my ninety-something year old grandfather, George Kupenski, straightening used nails, and then trying to straighten a few myself, was an example of the punishment of Sisyphus who endlessly rolled the large bolder up a hill, only to have to do it all over again after it rolled back down. He had been the king of Ephyra, known now as Corinth, and was being punished for his deceitfulness. I don't know why my grandfather and I were being punished with what seemed like an endless task. My grandparents, and even my own parents, never wasted anything. "Mend it, or do without it," was my father's motto. There was always something to build or fix in rural areas, so saving used nails for future projects was simply the correct way, and the smart way to live. He'd silently work there for hours and hours. I did too sometimes, but mostly I'd sit and watch just a while, a very short while. So, many times, after what seemed like an hour to me, he'd let me try to tap down the curves in some of the bent nails. Then, after I felt I could do it correctly whenever I needed to, I'd venture into the next room of the barn where the hay was stored, and climb up a shaky old ladder and into the hayloft. The back wall of the hayloft was where we had our outdoor basketball court.

It was in June when my cousin from Mary D, Pennsylvania came visiting. We toured my playing areas, including the barn, while the adults drank beer, ate pretzels, and brought each other up to date about local information, and what the extended family was doing. Grownups always talked about who was sick and who had died. Grownups must have been young like me once, I thought, so what happened to them? When did they stop playing? When did they get to be so joyless? Why so much talk about dead people?

Mary D was a small town just south of Tamaqua, where Ricky also had some cousins. The name of one town, Mary D, was so simple, and the other town's name, Tamaqua, sounded so strange. It could have been a place that Flash Gordon might have visited during his travels throughout the galaxy. The entire area survived on its coalmines, and it's where my Uncle Mike and I would drive to in his dump truck whenever he needed to restock his coal bins.

My cousin Jimbo, whose real name was James, loved to try the things I did all the time. We shot my bow and arrows. We walked along the ties of the railroad, and we played in the barn where we'd climb up to the hayloft, and jump down into a large pile of hay that lay waiting to be pitchforked up onto the loft.

"Sure we won't break out necks?" Jimbo asked the first time we were about to jump down into the pile of hay.

"I never did."

"Okay, you jump first. Show me the softest spot," he inquired.

"Watch," I shouted from the air as I jumped the fifteen feet down onto the hay pile below.

I was barely out of the way before he hit the hay in the exact spot I'd just landed on. If I hadn't quickly rolled to the floor, he might have flattened me.

We quickly tired of all the climbing up, but not the jumping down. After only six trips up, and then flying down, I hit a stick in the hay.

"What the heck is that?" Jimbo questioned.

I pulled it up a foot, and then another foot, but it just kept coming out of the side of the hay pile. It was the handle of a pitchfork. Some one had left it in the pile, with its sharp, deadly, forks slanting upward. Neptune is always seen with a three-pronged fork. The devil's fork might have also had three prongs, or maybe it has four prongs like the ones used to pitch hay. Four deadly sharp spikes facing upward toward the loft from where we jumped. If either of us had hit the pile a foot to the left of where we'd been landing, we would have been killed. Impaled. Stabbed to death by our own doing through someone else's stupidity. Tools, I'd been taught, were always put back in exactly the same place where they came from. Otherwise you'd spend hours looking for the tool when you needed it.

When my mother said, "Don' be stupid. Keep away from that," I now understood. I could easily be hurt if I did something stupid, or from someone else's stupidity. Stupid people do stupid things. If you were also stupid, then the other people's stupidity affected you even more. The world was far more dangerous than I had ever realized. That night, I dreamt about hitting that pitchfork. Some dreams should stay with you for a long time. Others, like seeing yourself impaled, should not.

Of course, being twelve meant that contemplating on safety after a near missed accident, was very short lived. We knew nothing about whatever Time had planned. In minutes, we left the barn to get my BB gun to go practice our marksmanship by shooting at the old broken windows in the closed factory where I'd recently learned about glass-block-bombs. It was Saturday, June 23, and we had all the time in the world.

My Daisy Red Ryder was my pride and joy. Just like Ralphie in *A Christmas Story*, we never worried about ricochet dangers. Holy smokes, we shot real guns; 22's at rats. We were just propitious, not smart, and Time must have wanted us around. That oddball brother of His, must have lingered near us too. Luck, I'm sure, got a kick out of that one. We'd missed the pitchfork, and no BB's ever ricocheted to hurt us. Sure, Anthony had a near-death experience, as he called it, with a hard, green tomato, and Billy Strusser's bee attack might have been deadly, but that was nothing compared to what would soon happen to Billy, but when Time grants you total freedom, even the freedom from rational thinking, you tend to throw caution to the wind.

The speed and distance the BB flies all depends on how many times you pump the handle on the gun. The pump was the piece under the barrel. We'd try eight pumps first. Shoot, then make note of its impact. Then, up it to ten pumps, and even to twelve or fourteen. The more you pumped, the harder it was to compress the air before firing. The harder you pumped, the faster the BB flew out from the rifle, and the more impact it had when it hit the target.

We were soon frontiersmen defending our campsite from Indians. Most of the windows had been broken for years, but pieces of glass were still set in the corners. They were our targets. Jimbo must have shot a dozen times before he hit a piece of glass. I was pretty good at it and hit glass every time I wanted to, so I began to hit the frame, and not break any more glass. I missed whenever he missed so he wouldn't feel bad. I don't know why, but I didn't want him to feel out of place. It was something you just picked up living in Milway. Some other kids from Milway weren't like that. Kenny, and his brother, Carl, had massive inferiority complexes as I much later came to understand. They were the only ones who ever teased and tried to humiliate other kids. But it really didn't matter much; they lived the furthest away from the center of town and seldom, if ever, joined us with our summer expeditions and projects.

Jimbo went home to Mary D the following morning. I didn't see him again for years. When he returned about four years later, he had grown up and had little or no summer left in him. I missed the summer Jimbo.

After Jimbo and his family returned to Mary D, we Milway guys all got together at Spitz's gas station right after supper, and played Kick-the-Can until almost dark, or until we heard, "Billy", or "Johnny", called out by our mothers. Parents paid attention to clocks; we never did. I figured a watch stopped at the number twelve for a reason, and that was because when you're twelve-years-old, you shouldn't think about anything else beyond that. There were twelve months in a year and I figured the twelfth year of these months must be special, must be the best one of all. I was right.

We'd play a number of different games. Sometimes we'd play up to three or four youthful games in the same day. The best was Kick-the-Can, and it combined Hide and Seek, fast running, Capture the Target, and Tag. We played Tag on the school's playground during the school year, but Kick-the-Can had to be played near dusk, at a time when things could disappear into the long shadows around barns and chicken coops. It was against some unwritten rule that it ever be played in the morning, or at mid-day. No, Kick-the-Can was a sunset game, and only for summer, and if you won, you were World Champion! There were always a lot of empty quart Texaco oil cans around the gas station. It was the same game my uncles said they played long before they were involved with World War II.

We, like them, made do with very little. We never bought a new baseball. We put electrical tape around the old torn one. We never got a net for our basketball court; we shot balls through just the iron frame, but Kick-the-Can was a game that demanded no bought objects, only an old discarded empty oil can. There were no requirements at all to play, except enthusiasm, and the ability to run. Every kid on earth could find an old empty can and play the same game. That's why we called ourselves World Champion when we won.

Whoever was "it," closed his eyes while we all hid. He'd then try to find us, and tag us to go to jail somewhere near the can. If any of the other guys got to kick the can before he could tag them, everybody went free. There were a lot of strategies involved: attacking without being tagged, and being as stealthy as possible were just a part of playing well enough to win. It was a summer ritual that was played during every single year when I was growing up. Kicking a can and kicking the bucket were two entirely different things. You learn about the second concept, and what that expression really means as you grow older and sadly forget about what being twelve was really like.

I don't see today's children playing many made-up games anymore. They have impact-free playgrounds. They'd never tie an old tire to a tree limb, and make a swing. They'd never straighten out crooked nails, or jump from a hayloft. Even the families, back then, who could afford to buy factory-made devices for toys, still let their children make, invent, and discover things to play with. I've never said that 1956 was better than 1986, or 2016. It was simply different, and it produced different kinds of people.

Only Time can pronounce the final decision on which year was His best. When it was so good that He'd let it slow way down, and linger on and on for as long as possible. The summer of 1956 was the longest summer ever recorded. That's true. Chance's older sister Sorrow, was nowhere to be found, but Joy, her younger sister, was spotted nearly everyday in the same buildings, fields, and woods where we played.

7-A

It would be many years later that I would read George Bernard Shaw's play, *Pygmalion*. My New York cousins, when visiting, told me that they saw *My Fair Lady* on Broadway at the end of March that year. They loved it, both the songs and the story. They'd hum the melodies from the show. I wonder now if they knew it was really *Pygmalion*.

At that time, I didn't know anything about it and even if I did, I wouldn't understand why someone would want to change a person from who they really are into something else? In college, I would learn that even Shaw took his idea from an ancient Greek legend. Who knows where the Greeks got it? It seems all the best stories were all used up a long, long time ago.

Time was flying by for me during the summer of 1956. I just wasn't paying any attention to it, and suddenly June became July. My parents said that Grace Kelly was a very lucky girl because she was becoming a real life Princess by marrying Prince Rainier of Monaco. Monaco, to me, was a mystic land, and I knew we couldn't get there by driving to it in our automobile. I read that the United States tested an H-Bomb on Bikini Atoll, which meant nothing to me at all. Firecrackers and glass blocks made the biggest explosions I knew. I thought French girls wore bikinis at the beach, and nobody, not a single one of my buddies, had any idea what an Atoll was.

After sunrise one Wednesday morning, I heard the morning missionaries of Milway, the same men who gathered everyday at the Post Office, say that IBM had made a one-ton hard drive with five megabytes that did away with needing punch cards. They said the machine covered sixteen square feet. I knew what punch cards were, but had no idea what an IBM was.

"Some day we'll all have a machine to do our calculating for us," said Sam De Ross.

"Never happen," responded Mayor Krokokos.

"You'll see. We'll have a hotel on the moon too," said Mr. De Ross.

God only knew what they were talking about. I don't even know why I remember their conversations, or why I can recall so many of their ambiguous comments.

"Egg prices keep going down, and I'll have to get out of the business," said Mr. De Ross.

"Everybody's into it now," answered the Mayor. "That's why they're down. Way too many eggs."

"We never thought there'd be too much of anything during the Depression, did we?" Mr. De Ross followed up.

"Some day there'll be too much of everything," replied the Mayor. "Even too many people."

Mr. Harry Bullkey was slowly approaching from where he'd left his car parked on the grass in the field where my historic igloo had been built. He caught the last two sentences and then added,

"There's never too much of anything. If you can't remember twenty-five-twenty-six years ago, then there's no hope for any of us."

I didn't expect any answer because I knew there never was such a time as twenty-five or twenty-six years ago. There's only now. I couldn't even recall any previous summer.

"That was different," responded the Mayor. "Nobody could make anything because nobody had any money. Can't ever happen again."

"Sure can," said Mr. De Ross. "All we've got to do is think it can't happen again, and it will. People caused the Depression, and people can do it again."

"Don't fret about it," said the Mayor. "From now on we'll make too much of everything, just like producing too many eggs. And the worst part about it is that some machine will do all the work. We won't even need people anymore."

Mr. Bullkey just smiled. He sold cars, not eggs. He was also the best skeet-shooter in America. He won a national championship once by just one hit more than his opponent out of one hundred shots. Milway was filled with really interesting people, but Billy and I ignored nearly everything except whatever project I was directing at the time.

As to what the Mayor had said, well, he was the Mayor. He must be right, I thought. So the last thing he said scared me a little. When I talked to Billy about what I'd heard, he said that it would be great if machines did all our work. Then we could play all the time.

That was a good point, I thought, but Billy, like me, had no concepts of a future. The only time you could ever be in is now.

I never knew that the price for eggs was listed each day in the papers I delivered. The only thing I read about in the paper was the baseball team rankings, and how the summer Olympics was about to start in Melbourne, Australia, wherever that was. No one from Milway was in it, or going there to watch. So we hosted our own Olympics. We used half a red brick for a shot-put, made two hurdles to run and jump over from old two-by-fours, and cut one long thin stick, about five feet long from Billy's high hedge row to use as a javelin. We did cut another tall hedge stick to use as a bar for our high jump. We set up two nearly rotten four-by-fours, taken from the old cow shed where they supported part of the roof, and we gave them a new life; a new purpose. We drove in a series of finishing nails one inch apart on the backsides of both pieces of lumber, and set the hedge stick, now our height bar, on the nails. After a successful jump, we'd move the bar up another inch to the next higher nail.

I was best at running and jumping. Ricky was best at throwing. What Billy lacked in natural ability, he made up for with effort. He was seldom last, but never first in anything. My younger cousin Billy tried them all, but wasn't big enough yet to compete very well with the older kids. His buddy Jackie, the Mayor's son, wasn't old enough either, but they at least tried. Milway kids would try anything.

The Milway Olympics didn't get any attention anywhere, and didn't last more than one morning, and two long, long afternoons.

After throwing the javelin, and measuring how far it went with my father's big tape measure, and then making a few hurdle runs with no competition, because no one else wanted to run and jump, we all went to buy frozen fudge bars at Mrs. Malatina's mini-mart, as we'd call it today. The next day, I ran and jumped the hurdles all by myself for the last time. Well, we quickly tired of the Milway Olympics even though Ricky broke his own shot-put record twice. I learned to roll over the high-jump bar, instead of just jumping straight forward over it, and got higher and higher with each jump, but we had nothing soft to land on, so by the second day, my side and back hurt way too much to try to break any more records.

I'll bet every twelve-year-old everywhere in the world sets up his own Olympics every four years ever since the Olympics began. Greek, Chinese, or Canadian; everywhere a twelve-year-old hears about the games, he'll replicate them.

We didn't care if we wasted a day playing our make-believe Olympics because it was a leap year. Wednesday the 29th had been added to February that year, and I knew we already had an extra day to waste. Since the Olympic events were held only every four years, none of us could remember the previous Olympics, and none of us could imagine even four days into the future let alone a full four years. Old man Time watched us, it seemed, with a deeper intensity, and maybe He was upset about us having an additional twenty-four hours, but He couldn't do anything about it.

8

If Tudor hadn't watched the *Lone Ranger*, and saw how he tied to a rope to a tree, and then pull the rope across a small passageway in the mountains, he'd never have tried to do it himself. Like the Ranger, Tudor tied a rope to a small red maple tree near Billy's house, and then pulled it across his driveway, which happened to go all the way around his house, and back out to the same road where it began on the other side of the house. Tudor then hid behind the hedge bush in the side yard just off the driveway. You could see him from my grandfather's tomato field, but he was impossible to spot coming down Billy's driveway.

The Lone Ranger did it to knock two bandits off their horses because they'd stolen his guns. He pulled it tight as the bandits galloped through the slender passageway. Both bandits caught the rope right across their chests, and fell backwards off their horses and onto the dirt. The Ranger ran out from his hiding place, recovered his, and their weapons, and tied them up for the trip into town and jail. Tudor's plan was miscalculated, and poor Billy Strusser paid for Tudor's failure to think ahead, and foresee any possible consequences.

"You guys bike up to Billy's storage building," instructed Tudor. "I'll get the rope ready, and all you have to do is let him pass you before he turns into the driveway. I'll wipe him right off his seat. Catch him in the chest, and lift him right into the air."

"Okay," answered Anthony.

Ricky and I hesitated to say anything. Chance, and either one of Her sisters could be peeking in on us.

My father had always taught me to think ahead, especially when we were rabbit hunting, and to anticipate what can happen. It's a skill every parent teaches, I thought. Tudor was a year older than Billy and me, and he told us how the cowboys on television hadn't been hurt, just shocked, so we went along with it. Even today, kids believe what they see on television or at the movies.

Ricky, Anthony, Billy, and I all rode up to Billy's father storage building where he loaded the trucks with his eggs that would be shipped to Atlantic City, and even up to New York. Not long after we got there, Ricky said let's race back to Billy's side yard, the same yard where Anthony nearly passed out from the rock-hard green tomato strike.

The four of us all rode neck and neck peddling fast at first, then slowing to coast. We passed Spitz's gas station, and then we let Billy pull just ahead of the rest of us.

"Second driveway," Anthony shouted as Billy was passing him.

I slowed down even more than any of the others did. Even though I usually could beat all of them in bike races, I dropped back to the last place. I dropped back to be sure if Tudor did knock Billy off his bike, I wouldn't hit him with my bike while he was getting up.

Billy was excited that he was ahead of us all, and suddenly he tried to make a final sprint into his driveway. He never saw Tudor behind the hedge. He never saw the rope pulled tightly across the driveway. Tudor hadn't figured the proper chest level, and Billy caught the rope right across his neck. It lifted him right off his bike seat. His phantom bike kept going all by itself way into his back yard nearly missing his garage before it fell with a rumbling sound against his Sear's-bought swing set. Anthony hit his brakes and slid pass where Billy was spread out on the ground. Ricky nearly ran him over as he lay perfectly still on the graveled driveway with his face up toward heaven. I had already slowed down, and simply rode off the driveway onto the grass near where Tudor was hiding.

"I think he's d-d-dead," stuttered Tudor.

Billy laid still. His opened eyes stared into the dead silence of the warm afternoon, into the heavens. It was so quiet that we could hear our hearts beating in our ears. Then, we heard him choking for air. The rope had caught him right across the throat. You could see the rope-burn mark across his neck. Like the Lone Ranger's bad guys, the fall hadn't really hurt him much, but it took so long for Billy to be able to take a painless full breath that we were all scared to death. None of us thought about how easily it could have broken his neck. Tudor took off for home when he heard Billy's mother coming out from their back door. Anthony told her that he fell off his bike, but that he was okay. He still had almost no color in his face, and I'm sure she thought we'd killed him.

"Oh my God," was all she said as she looked upon what she thought was the corpse of her dead son.

Billy had some blood on his lips, and he tried to tell his mother that he was okay. She helped him sit up, then get onto his knees, and finally to stand up before she told us all to go home. She helped him slowly walk into the house to put a cold compress across the reddish-brown rope-burn that you could see charred across the front of his neck. Had he been able to pedal faster, he just might have been killed.

Tudor didn't join in with us much after that for the remainder of the summer. He didn't even help dig when we started our biggest summer project. I'm sure he carried the fear of the moment with him for a long, long time. At least I hoped he did. Ricky and Anthony seemed to forget it quite quickly. Billy had the bruise mark on his neck for at least two weeks. When any of the other kids we played with asked him about it, he always told them that the outlaws tried to hang him, but he got away. None of the younger guys ever knew whether or not to believe him. The rope-burn mark mostly disappeared just before his next unbelievable tragic event while we were playing Knights. After that, there was an event where we both could have been impaled. I guess I was just fortunate. Billy wasn't. We were encouraged by Chance to try new things all the time whether Her absentminded cousin, Luck, was nearby or not.

I could sense how Time was watching us that sunny warm summer afternoon. I can recall how the crickets stopped chirping, no birds flew through the azure sky, no train went by, nor could you hear the sound of any automobile engines. I felt no wind on my face, so the screeching sound I heard must have been the grass growing, or maybe the new leaves on the trees bursting forth from their stems. Whenever you can't taste or smell, see or hear, and you just stand still touching nothing, you forget where you are. You become isolated from everything. Only later on, do you begin to recall what happened, or the really scary part, what could have happened.

*   *   *

My turn was next, but none of the other guys who almost killed Billy would be around when Chance put me to the test, and that nitwit brother of Time, Luck, almost got there too late. Only my brother Jimmy, who thought he'd killed me, but honestly, really had nothing to do with it, was there. It was all my own fault. I'd forgotten everything my father had ever said about looking and planning ahead, and then asking yourself, "What will happen if…" If you could teach everybody to use my father's phrase before they attempted to do things, the world might just be a far safer, happier place.

I saw Jimmy talking with my Uncle Mike just four days after Tudor's fiasco with Billy, the rope, and the bicycles. We didn't care what we ever saw the Lone Ranger do again. None of us wanted to be the Lone Ranger any more. Anyway, it was just after lunchtime when Uncle Mike told my brother that the keys were in the tractor. Next thing I knew, I could see him pulling out driving the old farm tractor with a disk harrow attached behind it. Mike had plowed the field behind Joast's house, the one next to Kupenski Bar, and right next to our Milway Baseball field. They would rotate the crops planted there, and this year it had been peas in the early spring, then, a crop of string beans had been harvested. I figured they wanted to get one more crop planted and harvested before winter's first frost, so Jimmy was driving the tractor over to level off the field after all the plowing had roughed it up. The disks are the same size as automobile hubcaps, but much thinner. They have a sharp edge all the way around. They're all slanted in a slightly different angle with a front row of six, and a back row of eight. They would slice the plowed chunks of earth into small pieces of dirt, and after two or three trips across the bumpy field, you'd have a level garden field that was all ready for the new seeds or baby plants to be inserted down rows into the freshly leveled field.

I rode my bike over to watch him work on the field. By the time I got there, he had already covered the entire field once, and was now making it even smoother with a second disking. Maybe I'd ride on the tractor with him a little before my newspapers were dropped off. There was a border of large old maple trees in a straight line from the bar to near the back of the field. A cluster of old pear trees stood, un-pruned, un-cared for, and simply forgotten about at the back of the field. I thought my uncles had planted them when they were boys, but Popeye, much later on, told me they were there already when he was growing up. They must have been planted by, or right after, Adam and Eve I figured. There's just no way to know how long ago things might have happened when Time takes his summer nap.

Well, I took off my sneaks and socks, and then I ran barefooted in the flattened moist earth behind the disk for a while. Then, when Jimmy slowed to make a turn, and could hear me over the tractor's engine, I asked if I could catch a ride.

"Sure," he yelled over the roar from the tractor's poor muffler.

"Where can I sit?" I asked him.

"Here," he pointed to the right fender over the four-foot high back tire.

"Okay. Great," was all I said.

I hopped on and rode down an entire row with him. He was well into working on the second disking when I got on, and I sensed he had other things that he wanted or needed to do, so he pushed the gas control arm forward and speeded up a little. It wasn't as rough after it had all been disked once already, so you could easily drive faster without bouncing as much. I liked the extra speed. I liked the dust we kicked up blowing behind us and not into our faces and eyes. I liked having my big brother all to myself even if it was a silent time we were spending together. Then, as I tried to move up higher on the fender, I slipped and fell directly in front of the right side large back tractor tire. I lay perpendicular to the tire, with my face down in the soft moist farm soil. He ran over me. It all happened in less than a second. The disks were about to follow and slice me into hundreds of pieces, but he stopped, and I heard the tractor's roar diminish. It seems that Time was hesitating; He couldn't decide. I remember hearing Chance calling to her older sister, Sorrow, that She should come at once. Then all I heard was Jimmy's voice asking me something.

The weight of the tractor's large back wheel pushed me down into the soft, moist, dark earth. I sank easily because the ground was so soft, and still wet from yesterday's rain shower. Had it been hard and dry, the tire would have crushed the small of my back, just below my bottom ribs, and just above the start of my hipbones. Had it been in front with the smaller front tires, but with all the weight of the engine on the front axle, I'd have quickly died. As it were, even though it was my stupidity to change my position on a moving tractor, the incalculable odds were with me, and I pulled my face and neck up out of the dirt to get a better breath. I'd also fallen onto one of the wetter spots in the field and sank easily providing little resistance to the crushing weight of the big wheel.

Now, even I knew you don't move an accident victim, but Jimmy was really frightened. He grabbed me by both arms, and pulled me slowly away from the tractor, and onto the clean grass at the edge of the plowed field.

"Can you breathe?" he quietly asked.

"Yes."

"Can you move your legs? Do you feel you toes?"

I told him I could feel my toes and legs, but I couldn't yet roll over onto my back. I didn't think I could sit up at all. Neither of us had any idea if anything inside was crushed. Jimmy probably thought about that more than I did. So he just let me lie there and rest.

Trying to ride on a tractor, on a tractor's fender that is, and not in the seat, was what people do who never think ahead. I had acted stupidly. It was summer, and I was twelve, so Time let me be irresponsible, while His brother Luck provided a safety net; the soft moist soil. I was blessed. I got time to grow up. Time's crazy brother, Luck, must have been on the tractor's other rear fender. There's no other explanation. Chance quickly disappeared, but Her sister faded away ever so slowly.

I could feel my breathing getting faster as I realized what had just happened. I couldn't remember falling at all, just lying there with the tire on my back as Jimmy jerked the tractor forward, and stopped short of the disk hitting me. He had about two and a half feet to play with before the disk would begin slicing me into hundreds of pieces.

He helped me roll over. I didn't feel any pain anywhere. I found it a little hard to breathe, but that, I assumed, was from being scared. Nothing was broken or crushed. Time had cut me a break. I know his simpleton brother, Luck, was somewhere nearby, but Time was the only entity I could feel watching me now. I had dirt in my nose and eyes, but I relaxed some as soon as I pulled my legs up, and put my arms around them. Then, as I lay back down again, I heard Jimmy say, "Don't tell Mom. Don't say anything. I'll deliver your papers for you. Just rest until you can walk again."

That was the only time Jimmy ever helped me with the paper route. Even when I was sick, and it was raining, he was unable, or unavailable, to help. Of course I'd keep this secret; he was doing my work for me, and I guessed that brothers, no matter what the distance between them, don't betray each other.

It wasn't until years later, when I worked in construction during my college summer breaks, that I knew my lower back wasn't as strong as it should be. Then, even years after that, I had an MRI that showed some squeezed-together vertebrae, and there was one disk even bulging out. To avoid lower back pain, nowadays, I lay on the floor and stretch, and every time I do, I remember being nearly buried alive in the wet garden soil underneath the weight of the tractor's big rear wheel.

Not long after that summer, Jimmy graduated High School, and left for the Navy; I wasn't even in Junior High yet. On his return visits, he exposed me to classical music, Jazz, and some artwork. Jimmy's college friends were artistic. Today, he is an artistic woodcarver, carving really beautiful wooden vases and bowls. My mother did beautiful flower arrangements, all picked from flowers that she planted in our own back yard, and my father created art with his stone and brickwork. Growing up in Milway meant you didn't need New York museums; we had everything you ever needed to learn, everything was there that you needed to know. Athens, Paris, London, or New York had absolutely nothing over Milway.

*   *   *

I was really stiff the next morning after I was run over by the tractor, and I had to deliver the newspapers by myself the following day, but the pedaling on my bicycle actually helped, and it made my lower back feel better. You're always the sorest the day after you get hurt, and the back of my legs hurt down to my knees. I could never figure out why that foolish old Luck let His cousin Chance incite me to try moving on that tractor fender. Maybe Her older sister, Sorrow, encouraged Her to do it?

My mother was busy washing Ball quart canning jars when she asked me why I was walking funny. I said that I fell off my bike into some sand. No big deal. She just shook her head and walked away.

I told her I was fine because we'd soon be going for peaches. I loved to help pick them. I'd always find and eat the biggest one I could spot before I began to help fill the half-bushel wooden baskets that we'd take along with us.

Saturday, July 28 was a bit early for ripe edible peaches, but not too early for cooking and canning them as preserves. The still-hard peaches were better for making preserves. We picked some to take home and test them. We'd repeat everything the following Saturday, August 4. It was time to put-up peaches, so off we drove to East Vineland to capture some golden rays of the summer sunshine that had been taken prisoner by the peach trees. Each peach was like a summer day. Each peach held the sunlight of a day that I had already lived through. It may have been from the day the bees stung Billy, or the day we put pennies on the railroad track. Maybe the peach I was biting into held some of the sunshine from the day we dropped glass blocks, or the day we lit firecrackers down at the gravel pits. Picking was easy. My mother would close the Post Office at noon on Saturdays, and we'd pick four full baskets before two o'clock. Knowing what previous day's sunshine we were taking home was the hard part.

Each Jersey peach was bigger than a baseball. They were golden-amber with cherry red splashes of color all over them. The man who owned the trees said that New Jersey was the fourth largest producer of peaches in the nation. That seemed like an awful lot of peaches to me. As I grew and met different people, I was always surprised to learn that their moms didn't preserve summer peaches for the approaching winter. We had so many of them that I just assumed that every kid my age experienced the same things I did. Since then, I've also been wrong about a lot of other things.

I learned that peaches were planted not too far west of Milway in the 1600's. If there were any kids back then, they must have enjoyed them as much as I did.

The hardest part began when we got back home, and again all day Sunday. Each peach had to be skinned very carefully so as not to lose too much of the peach's sweet flesh. They were cut in halves, and some into quarters. They had to be heated in the pressure cooker, and quickly transferred to the sterile quart Mason jars. The jars had been carefully washed that morning, and lined up all ready and waiting to be filled. Dozens of quart Mason jars were lined up along the edge of the sink. After each one was topped off with peach slices, they patiently waited to cool down, and then each thin tin lid had to be checked to be sure they had sealed properly. Putting up preserves is an ancient art. My mother was the best peach artist in town.

As the hot expanded-air cooled down, it created a slight vacuum in each jar. Normal air pressure pushed the lid down onto a tight enclosure. The now-filled quart jars were sealed, and only had to wait for the coming winter to once again be freed. They were Helen's gift of some long lost warmth on icy days. They were served cool, directly from the refrigerator in tiny bowls, but I knew that each slice held the heat of summer even if there was snow on the ground outside. They were my mother's promise that summer would once again return, and provide a freedom that only adolescents can know. Each quart jar of peaches imprisoned Time, and it seemed that He didn't mind it one bit.

When all the filled quarts were back down to room temperature, it was my job to carry two at a time, or four in a cardboard box, down our cellar steps, and line them up like solders all in a row. Quart after quart of golden peaches… all standing at attention waiting until the hour came when I awoke in the early darkness, and went to sleep not so long after sunset. Winter. Each quart jar was holding a part of some past day's summer sunshine. They would sleep quietly, in the cool darkness of our cellar, until I was once again back in school, and frost would whiten the grass, or ice would hang from our front porch roof, or snow would make summer seem as far away as the furthest star in the galaxy.

My mother could show Time a thing or two. She knew how to keep it from disappearing. Each spoonful recaptured every fort building, every bike ride, all the Kick-the-Can competitions, and every firecracker moment from the day school let out to the very end of summer. You shouldn't talk with your mouth full, but every single slice of every single peach had a story to tell.

9

A quart jar of peaches was all it took to time-travel. My mother's peaches were frozen in time. We waited for icy weather, and fewer hours of sunlight to release a captured day from the previous summer. A sunny day that was imprisoned in a Mason jar of peaches. Whenever we began to feel the days getting cooler, my father and I looked forward to an after-dinner dish of sweet, golden peaches. However, while I tolerated the current blistering hot summer days, and before it was time to open any quart jars of mummified time, I recalled two record-breaking freezing weeks during the past winter. Thinking about it helped me stay cool. It was during the previous winter, when all the guys in our Milway group were snowed in by a massive nor'easter. Time didn't come to a complete stop back then, but it really slowed down. As each day grew hotter and hotter, we tried to recall how cold it was during last winter's massive snowstorm. There was no school for three days, and then we had a weekend. For five straight days we escaped the classroom. Time was toying with the freedom of summer; He gave winter some of the freedom of summer because all of our responsibilities ceased. Yes, that's what freedom really is.

After a day and a half of a continuous snowfall, we had over twenty inches of moist marshmallow that we couldn't roast on a stick over a fire. It was only good for making snowballs. My mother had me so bundled up that I could hardly walk around enough to push and shovel snow into an icy white wall where I knew we'd have the biggest snowball fight in the complete history of Milway. The field between my house and the railroad tracks was the perfect spot. Open, safely off the nearest road, and visible to everyone who wanted to join in, like Flander's Field, it invited every snow soldier to meet his fate. In my mind, I saw all the boys of Milway becoming either Athenians or Spartans, and we'd use snowballs instead of swords to fight our own Peloponnesian War. I'd be Pericles, but I had no memory of where I'd ever learned about him or either of the Greek city-states. It had to be those books that opened their pages to me every night before going to sleep. Dozens of books that were filled with words that sprang up into my eyes, and raced deeply into my brain. I thought with those words, and they gave me ideas.

Smack! I felt the first snowball hit my back. Billy Strusser was the first guy to venture out and join the war. Ricky, Anthony, Tudor, my cousin Billy, and even Sonny's daughter, Patty, plowed through every obstacle to get to our battlefield. We really didn't form sides as I'd hoped to do; we simply squeezed clumps of snow in our cold wet gloves as fast as possible, and fired at whomever was the closest. When we finished making and throwing one frozen cannon ball, we quickly made another snowball and fired back at anybody we thought had hit us.

"Hey, no headshots," shouted Patty.

Girls…

"Yo! Not so hard," declared Ricky. Tudor packed his snowballs like mortar, and if it hit you in the legs, it really hurt.

My youngest cousin, little Gary joined up with my other cousin, Billy Layzan, and this youngest pair of snowball warriors also quickly joined in. We could see Carol standing on the front steps of the Milway hotel across the tracks, but she couldn't tell that we already had a girl battling with us, so she remained where she would be safe.

Snowball fights never really lasted very long. One shot caught Patty on the side of her face, and a lot of snow got into her hair under her hood. She had to leave. She shivered with the icy cold snow in her hair as she tracked back across the railroad tracks and toward her home. Tudor blasted Anthony with a rock-hard white projectile, and then turned to run home with Anthony shouting after him, "I'll fill your pants with snow for that one. You wait till I catch you. In your pants. I swear!"

Billy took the last shot from Ricky, and then he walked forward asking me what else did I think we could do?

Well, we'd been thinking about some major constructions ideas for the coming summer, like building forts, so I said, "Let's build a snow fort." Then, I added, "No, an igloo." Both Billy's and Ricky's eyes widened.

There was a few seconds of silence as they both looked at each other trying to recall what an igloo was.

"Great!" shouted Billy, as he broke the dead silence.

"We'll need snow blocks, lot and lots of them. Everyone go get a cardboard box, and meet right here after lunch, Okay?" I asked after giving instructions.

"You bet," said Ricky. "I've got one in the cellar. Old wine box I think."

"Okay. Right after lunch," said Billy.

And that is how the second largest construction project we ever worked on came about. The largest project happened near the end of the following summer, months before the days once again shortened, and the wild geese flew by heading south. But long before that future summer project could ever begin, we got hit with the biggest snowstorm anyone in Milway could ever remember. So, months before what we would construct on that very field, we had to take advantage of what we were blessed with right then; tons of snow. Even with all the exaggerated conversations that were orated on the porch of the Post Office by all the old-time philosophers in town, no previous snowfall seemed to compare with this one. No one could recall so much snow falling so quickly. It would take more than a day to clear off the roads, so we knew that school would be closed for a while.

We all ate our peanut butter and jelly sandwiches as quickly as possible, and then sourced up some cardboard boxes. Then, we all met back at the field in front of the Post Office to begin building Milway's first ever igloo, a real Eskimo igloo, one we could stand up in, and maybe spent the night like we did during our summer campouts. We sleep in our backyards, and even in the nearby woods during the summer, so why not spend a night inside the safety of an igloo.

We had four boxes, but only two were about the same size. I got Ricky started packing snow in each box, patting the sides of the box to help the snow-block free itself from the cardboard, then turning the cardboard box upside down to drop out the snow block. I told them to use the close-by snow first. We made ten blocks from a circled area I marked out, and then Billy brought them to me to place the snow-blocks in a circle.

The circumference was larger than the tepee Billy and I had built later that year, right at the start of summer.

I suggested that the opening shouldn't face north because the North wind would blow right inside the doorway opening we'd have to leave in the wall. We completed an almost perfect full circle, and then removed three snow blocks on the southwest side. We took those three snow blocks that we removed from the first row, and placed them onto the second course, and thought we were making good time. We would finish the project quickly. No such luck. It was cold. Our gloves were wet. Tiredness came on us faster than the passenger trains that flew by on the nearby railroad. We never thought working in the cold would take so much out of us.

As the afternoon went on, it seemed to take longer and longer to pack the boxes with fresh moist snow, pack them tightly with our hands, empty them near our building site, and then place the snow blocks onto the circular wall of snow. We tired very quickly. Even worse, two of our snow block forms, our cardboard box forms, were soaking wet, and they began to fall apart. Also, unlike during summer, four o'clock was not mid afternoon. Instead, by four o'clock it was nearly sunset. We all agreed to return in the morning as we watched the whiteness of the frosty sun linger just above the tree line to the western limit of Milway.

I remember not knowing how cold my hands were until I was inside, and I took off my gloves. My fingers were all pink. My mother ran cold water over them until I could feel the coldness of the water. She told me that you could use warmer water only after you could feel again; otherwise, you could damage your blood vessels and your skin. To this day, I've never checked to see if that were true, but mom's words were gospel absolutes when you were a kid.

"If your fingers freeze, we'll have to cut them off," she said.

I instantly knew I'd need an extra pair of gloves for tomorrow. Still, her words scared me, and I had a nightmare about being fingerless with just two palms to push things around. I'd done other dangerous things, had frightful things bite, hit, and sting me, had accidents too, but I never had a nightmare about any of those things, only about what my mother had said about me losing my fingers. I guess that's why I remember her comments so well.

By the time I finished breakfast the next morning and got outside, Ricky was already there with a new dry cardboard box. He'd just starting shoveling snow into it when I said, "Good morning," to him.

"It ain't packing like yesterday," he answered without any morning gesture of obeisance.

Billy was just arriving when I figured out that the icy night had re-frozen the snow. It was less damp. It was almost like fine powder, the kind of snow skiers really like, but it was no good for we snow-block makers.

"We got to wait until the sun makes it wetter," I stated.

"Okay," Billy said. "Let's go up to my house and look for more boxes."

My cousin Gary, too young to work very hard, but old enough to hunt for boxes, came over and asked what we were building. Ricky told him it was an igloo, and that we were all going to get more boxes to make snow blocks. "Help us find some," he told Gary.

We three big guys headed up past Billy's chicken coops to where they stored their chicken feed. We were in luck. We found two clean, dry cardboard boxes about the same size as the ones we had used the day before. It took us over an hour to look everywhere, and then trek back to the icy construction site. Anthony was there by then packing the now moist snow into the two boxes from yesterday; the only two that had stayed together. The sun was working its magic so the snow was beginning to stick better. By lunchtime, we had four rows of snow blocks completed and properly set in place.

We packed the four boxes and made four more blocks, and then we set the boxes on their sides to absorb more sun and dry out as much as possible as we all headed home for lunch. We knew we could make snow blocks faster as the day warmed up and gave us a better building material.

After lunch, Gary joined us again. Carol came from the Hotel and worked for a little while. Neil stopped by to see what we were doing after we had the wall up to just over four feet high. He told us that we'd never get it to curve in, and then he left without providing any help at all. I sent Gary over to Kupenski's Bar to ask for empty wine or beer cases. He carried four back, and then helped all of us make a few more snow blocks. Gary said that the men, who were all construction workers and jobless during most of the icy winter, were watching us build the igloo through the bar's front window. Gary said that when they asked him what we were doing, he said that he told them we were building the biggest igloo ever built in Milway, maybe anywhere. They all laughed and said, "Good luck with that one".

As soon as we had seven or sometimes eight blocks ready, Ricky and I would begin to set another row all the way around, but this time we began to slant them in a little toward the inside center. That left about two inches of space on the outside between the newly placed snow blocks, and the course that was already there. Anthony was the tallest amongst us, so he shoveled loose snow into that opened space, and all around the open joint for each new snow block that we set curving inward along the wall of snow blocks.

Each course slanted inward even more, and we all hoped they'd freeze together quickly before they fell in. Then, I suggested to Anthony that he push in the snow, and pack it in with the shovel handle. It worked. We had enough blocks made to do three more courses that would all slant inward at an ever-greater angle until they created the complete dome of our igloo. After slanting the blocks inward, we realized we needed one less block for each new course as the circle of snow blocks became smaller and smaller. The circumference continued to shorten faster with each new course that curved inward.

"Billy. Come with me," I shouted. "We need to get something to stand on from now on."

"I've got a small step-ladder in our garage," he answered.

"Great. Go get it. I'll look in our shed," I replied. "Keep making snow-blocks," I said to Ricky.

"Gary, go see if there's any more cardboard boxes that we can use over at the bar. These are almost falling apart," I commanded. "And watch for trucks crossing Tuckahoe Road." He was younger than the rest of us. Telling anyone of the younger guys to be careful always made us feel more like a grownup.

I headed to the shed where we kept our lawnmower. Surprisingly, I was aware that the lifeless machine seemed to be lonely. Really, the lawnmower was cast in an aura of isolation, of uselessness, or wanting to be needed. It seemed lonely to me. It was one fleeting moment of grownup thinking, and I didn't like it, not one bit. I'd have thought it would have enjoyed winter the most, when it could rest all by itself, and was not being pushed around all the time. Thankfully, this entire mental episode lasted only a few seconds. I did wonder if Chance's older sister, Sorrow, could affect a machine. I made a quick decision that it couldn't, and then just forgot about the mower. I needed something to stand on to reach the final snow block courses, and be able to close in the igloo ceiling. That was my mission, and I had no time to contemplate irrational emotions.

I dragged out from behind the mower, a small table that would be just the right height to stand on, and work from, for the next two courses of snow-blocks running around our igloo wall. By the time Billy got back, it was getting dark. Gary returned with just two boxes, so we made only five more blocks, and then quit for the day. We said we'd start early the next morning, and then we left to go home and get warm, give a progress report to parents, and anxiously wait until the following frozen morning. It was supposed to get colder and maybe snow again before the cold spell broke, so we knew we had to work faster starting the next morning.

I fell asleep picturing the igloo completed. We were camping out in it overnight. I awoke from my dream with both feet sticking out from under the covers, and the icy air coming in from the just-cracked-open window, was swirling around the room, and then settling on my naked toes. Wow, I thought to myself, the blocks will hold tight tonight, and it'll all be so frozen tomorrow that we can close in the top before any of the sidewalls cave in. I began to sense success. Each day we breathed in fresh, clean Arctic air, filled with oxygen molecules that may have already passed through the lungs of Indians, or explorers. We exhaled a warmer breath filled with memories that were carried away on the icy air to some far off place where other twelve-year-olds were working to build their own castle or fort. I doubted that anyone else would be building an igloo, at least not in South Jersey.

It was hot Quaker Oats again for breakfast. My mother didn't mind us working stupidly outside in the freezing weather because for a few rare days, she was able to easily keep an eye on me from the Post Office window. She could also see the entire gang of Milway Eskimos. The igloo was out in the field directly in front of the Post Office, which was once a section of a large living room in the front part of our house. That room was split in half while still attached to our house so it would have a lobby where people could open their mail boxes, and an office where mail was sorted, stamps sold, packages collected, and it also had enough room in that office section of the Post Office to keep all the government accounting books. All the Post Offices that we ever saw were part of someone's home back then. That is, every rural Post Office was part of someone's home.

"Don't let your gloves get wet," she ordered as I was heading out the door. I could still taste the butter she put on the oatmeal. I'd be warm enough, and could work as long as I wanted to, as long as I didn't get too wet.

Like every other boy growing up anywhere in the world, I replied in full agreement with my mother's command, "I won't."

Ricky was there first again. He shoveled snow into the frozen boxes. By now, we had to walk further and further away from our igloo to get good snow to make a block. He carried one box back near the entrance, patted its sides, and turned it over. Out came the first vanilla ice cream-colored snow block of the day. As soon as he finished making a second one, I jumped up on the table inside the circle of snow, and started placing another row of the icy snow-blocks all the way around the igloo's wall. Now, it took only five and a half blocks on this upper course to complete the circle, not ten blocks. Making half a block was easy. You'd pack the cardboard box with snow and make a full block, then, using a wide snow shovel, you'd simply slice the block in half. We had a number of half blocks lying near the entrance waiting to be used to fill in the smaller rows as the top curved inward more and more. It really looked like a church dome by now, as it curved inward at an ever-greater angle. Once we plugged in the open space above, all the blocks would push against each other and none could fall inward. An igloo is its own flying buttress. Its curved walls are its own support. Brilliant engineering. The early Eskimos seemed to have understood the concept of the Gothic architecture's flying buttress. However, instead of extending an exterior support, they incorporated the curved concept that supported a vaulted roof right into the sides of the walls they built for their homes. We where closing it in faster and faster and had to be careful not to make a mistake by rushing too much to finish the job. At the same time, we had to get the final snow block in quickly to tie the opposite side walls together directing the force from the weight of all the blocks back toward the ground, and not have any part of a wall simply cave in. Anthony got there just in time to fill in the last spaces around the entire seventh and eight courses on the outside. Men making their daily Post Office visit now began to shout things over to us.

"Looking good," yelled Bam.

"You'll be done by noon," said the Mayor. "Then you can all go home, and do some real work."

Harry Bullkey said, "Biggest igloo I've ever seen!"

"Biggest in the world," answered Ricky.

I briefly wondered just how many igloos Mr. Bullkey had ever really seen. Grown-ups tend to forget how kids tend to take all their words as actual facts.

Mrs. Strusser walked to the Post Office to mail some checks and saw it for the first time. "Billy told me it was a big igloo, but I had no idea how big it really was," she shouted to us.

"It's really warm inside," Billy yelled back to his mother already presenting the idea that it would be safe to spend the night in the igloo. Kids knew you had to lay the groundwork out early if you wanted your parents to agree to things that don't always seem sensible. "No wind gets in, and it stays warm," he added.

Mrs. Strusser ignored him as she went inside to mail her envelopes.

*   *   *

So off and on during the morning, as we closed in the final three courses, we had to stop working on the wall to answer and make replies to the men of Milway who, I'm sure, all wished they could skip work and help us complete our task. Each of them would have liked to maybe spend one night inside the igloo too. Using Billy's stepladder, I set the last three-block course leaving only one hole facing the cloudy silver-gray sky above. It was the final moments when the heavens could peer down into the igloo. The walls had held together and remained upright. I knew that numbskull, Luck, must have been in the area, and his brother, Time, had lengthened the day for us to be able to work just a little longer.

Ricky told Anthony, who just finished making another block to use the snow shovel and cut off about four inches. We'd used all the snow surrounding the igloo by then, and had to walk nearly sixty feet out into the field to get additional material to pack into our boxes to make the snow blocks. Billy walked out and picked it up, gave it to Ricky who handed it up to me, and I just pushed it up into the final opening. It stuck to every side. The only light coming in now was subdued gray light coming in through the doorway opening. The four-foot extension entrance should be long enough to stop any icy air from blowing directly inside the full central chamber of the igloo. You had to bend way over, or better yet, crawl through the four-foot entrance to get into the main vaulted dome. Inside you could easily stand up. A fully-grown man could also stand upright, even reach up with his arms without touching the highest part of the ceiling.

Billy slid out the ladder and started to take it home. "See you later," he shouted to all of us.

I pulled out the little table, and suggested we finish making the snow-blocks we'd need for the top curved part of the igloo's entrance before we break for lunch. Ricky agreed, and as I carried the table back to my father's shed, the guys quickly walked deeper into the field to make more blocks so we could complete the igloo's entrance. Some blocks started to fall apart when dumping them out of their forms because the cardboard boxes were now so wet and weakened that their sides couldn't hold the snow together. The area was littered with broken pieces of newly wet or older frozen cardboard. We went through every single cardboard box that Milway had to offer.

Three blocks went on each side going up to just three and a half feet high. Then we curved in the remaining two courses of blocks creating a smaller arched way over the entrance. I then used the snow shovel to round off the square blocks outside edges. We did it. It made me think of the Taj Mahal with its alabaster white walls reflecting India's brilliant sunshine. Our igloo had the frozen wintry light reflecting off its sides and dome. We'd built the first and final igloo that Milway would ever see.

As Gary collected all the little pieces of cardboard litter, Ricky and I carried off all the wet, broken cardboard boxes to my father's garbage area in our back yard. Billy returned just in time to help Anthony and me pack snow into all the open spaces where every block slanted inward. When we finished, the outside had no ridges remaining. The outside walls where a smooth curvature. We all stepped back toward the Post Office side of my house and quietly stared at the igloo. Then, without saying anything to each other, we all left for home and some warm food. I was certain that all my buddies felt the same joy as I did. Chance's younger sister danced among us. We found it hard to believe that we'd actually completed what we set out to do.

I remember the chicken soup and grilled cheese sandwich I had to celebrate the conclusion of the icy construction project. Life is filled with memories of such tiny things; maybe they're really the most important things? If they weren't, you'd never remember them. I realized that for me, and maybe Ricky and Billy too, the building of the igloo was more important than seeing it finished. As we all grew older we learned that the anticipation of some things is always better than the conclusion. Decorating and waiting for a prom is always better than the prom itself. It's the same for holidays like Christmas, and even weddings.

*   *   *

After lunch we searched for and found three old rugs for covering the solid ice floor inside the igloo. Everywhere we'd been walking during the construction was now packed as hard as stone. I found an old blanket in the barn, and that became the first floor cover. We put the three rugs on top of the blanket. In no time at all, we had enough material on the icy floor of the igloo to sit on. Billy and I planned to sleep over in the igloo like we did in our summer tent, but both our parents said we'd freeze to death, and they strictly forbid it. That was one of the very few times I can ever recall my mother ever forbidding me to do something. She knew that learning to survive comes from failures and making mistakes, but freezing to death would not be a learning experience.

When we explained how native Inuits and Eskimos did it all the time, well, both our parents said that we were not Eskimos; it was a point well made, and we could not argue against their observation. We weren't Eskimos, just Milway kids.

There was a very light snow that night that continued into the next morning; the igloo stood out like a Taj Mahal of pure, ivory-white marble projecting in an alabaster field of fresh, clean new snow. The building in Agra, India had been built as a mausoleum, so maybe our parents were correct in preventing us from staying in it all night in sub-freezing temperatures.

Everyone who came to the Post Office over the next few days, walked into the field, peeked into the igloo, and made amazing comments about it. A few of the wives even bent over and worked their way into the igloo. By the weekend, nearly every Milway citizen had visited the igloo. Even people driving by to Milltown or to Ways Cove slowed down to check it out, and some strangers even stopped to check out the tiny spot in Milway that had suddenly become a landscape of Alaska.

"Amazing!" exclaimed Mrs. Penerotti.

"Don't get caught inside when it starts to melt," was all that my mother, and my Uncle Mike said. They were right about that. The frozen snow blocks were really quite heavy, and if the entire wall fell in on you, well, you'd be in serious trouble.

My father, who really knew and understood construction, was also pleased with the job we'd all done. "We've got a lot of future block layers in Milway," he said.

The cold spell lasted another four days before temperatures rose above freezing for an entire day. But the sun did little damage to the igloo. Including the weekend, we had had a five-day break from reading, writing, and arithmetic. Snow assimilated directly from a solid into a gas. The roads, by then, were in good shape, and some grass was showing in the field around the igloo, where we'd removed over a foot of snow to make the blocks, but the structure stood sturdy like the Rock of Gibraltar.

"I bet it'll last till summer," Billy said on the first day that we had to return to school after our unexpected break.

"Maybe,' I said. "Just maybe." I was more proud of having built it than any pleasure you'd get from thinking about how long it would last. I never liked thinking about the past, and seldom wasted any time contemplating the future. Now, was all there ever really was. We were told about people who had died in the past, but we didn't have any concept about death. We were taught that death was in everyone's future, dogs, cats, even people, but that too was meaningless. I left both those exercises to Time because He knew more about both of them than I ever could. I was happy that Time let his simpleton brother, Luck, join us when we forced the last snow block into the dome. Their cousin, Chance, encouraged me to do it, and I did. The arched roof was completed. Nothing fell in. No blocks collapsed. I heard Chance's sister, Joy, sing with pleasure at our accomplishment. I may have even seen Her reflection on the shiny ice in front of the igloo, but I can't swear to it. I am certain that I heard her giggle when I told everyone how pleased I was that we could do it.

Ricky too suggested it might never melt, at least not until summer. We all create our best memories. "It's like a rock," he said after patting the inside wall two days after we'd finished it, two days before the temperature rose above freezing. We'd all stop by on our way to school, and again as soon as we walked home from our classes, and changed into our old, warmer outside clothes. More than once my mother provided cups, and made hot chocolate for us to savor while sitting on the frozen carpets inside the igloo. Participation dwindled to just Ricky, Billy, and me. Finally, it was just Billy and I who used it as another fort not knowing that it was simply youth that was the real fortress from the outside world.

The igloo slowly became a backup play site after most of the snow had disappeared. The grassy field had only some isolated icy spots from our stomping down the snow during our snow-block making, but the fully compacted igloo was frozen together, and lasted another week and a half after every other flake had melted away.

The more we lost interest in it, the faster it faded. It was like old friendships, or old unused toys. They simply faded into time and disappeared. Sometimes they reappeared, briefly, like the igloo episode always does whenever any of us is telling someone about the greatest summer of our Milway lives, and the winter that came before it. Every summer story we've ever told since we were twelve, had to include this single wintry item.

As the igloo melted more and more, and after we all began to neglect it, I think it's possible that the lonely igloo had more in common with the unused lawn mower than anyone could ever imagine.

9-A

My front yard was very small. My grandparents, my mom's mother and father, with an aunt and three uncles, lived directly across the street. The western side of our yard was filled with my mother's lilacs, and the eastern section had an enormous spruce tree growing almost three times the height of the electrical lines, some of which, ran through its limbs. My mother could never remember when the tree wasn't there, and she was born in the house right across the street, my grandparents' place. All around the giant spruce was periwinkle with its deep green leaves that never turned brown in winter, and tiny purple flowers that introduced each new spring and summer to the world with their explosive color. The periwinkle grew all around the tree in a nearly perfect circle.

Billy and I used the grass that grew between the periwinkle and the shoulder of the road as our outdoor summer's couch. On many of the warm midsummer nights, we'd get together again after our evening meals. We'd lie back, with our bellies full, and stretch out near the spruce tree on my grassy front lawn, and look up at the stars as they began to fill the summer night. If we sat upright, we'd be looking directly at my grandparent's house. Instead, we laid back with out heads touching the green lawn, and focused on the blackness of the northern sky. We'd see the very ends of a few spruce limbs, and nothing else but stars. In the northwestern sky, the seven stars in the Big Dipper were the easiest to spot. My father said that as a boy, back in Ireland, they called them King David's Chariot. In France, that star cluster was referred to as the Great Chariot, and they are called The Plough, in the British Isles. In the bible: Amos 5:8 calls our Big Dipper, "the seven stars". Those seven stars are just the brightest part of the complete constellation Ursa Major. These specifics were the kind of things we learned in school. It's specific stuff, the real facts, that takes all the magic out of the world.

I'd lie on my back, and Billy and I would talk about how far away we thought the brightest stars were, if we'd ever send a rocket out there like the ones Flash Gordon flew in, which one God might be on, and then change the subject and wonder if we'd ever get old like our grandfathers.

We'd discuss history, evolution, anthropology, and theology without ever knowing we were philosophers. We spoke in the most basic terms. Even though Time rested there too, right along side us on the same carpet of summer-green grass. He never contributed very much to our discussions.

Maybe Time whispered that it was *Dubhe* and *Merak*, the two brightest stars in the Big Dipper, that formed a line pointing to *Polaris*, the North Star, which was used by all our ancestors to help find their way back home in the dark. Maybe I just imagined that He whispered it because Billy never heard Him. I told Billy that Cave Men could find that same star that we were looking at, and they too, must have wondered about what they really were, and must have talked about them during warm summer nights just as we were doing. During the freezing winter sky, during igloo building time, the Big Dipper had moved across the black sky to another location. Cave Men noticed that too, I'm sure. We've destroyed the beauty of the night sky with all our backyard floodlights, and so much street lighting now. Modern Milway kids never look up at the night sky any more. There's almost nothing left to see; nothing left to wonder about.

On a really still breeze-free evening, you could hear music coming from the jukebox in Kupenski's Bar across the railroad tracks, about two football fields west of my house. We had great hearing back then, and we could hear insects sharing concerns with each other, and we'd also hear the summer air sneaking through the tall grass, which sounded different than when it flowed over gravel or over a newly plowed field, and every once in a rare while, we'd hear Time and Luck arguing with each other. At least I did.

Billy said, "You know, the Cave Men had somewhere to hide from the ice in winter, and a cool place to be in during the fiery heat of late summer. You know, before Indian summer, I mean when it's so hot you can't sleep. Dog days hot."

"But we don't have any caves in Milway."

"I know. I wish we did," he pondered.

"If those stars are just big balls of fire," I continued, "they must really be hotter than every day in August put together."

"Hotter than an oven. Hotter than a bonfire," Billy concluded.

Billy was correct about how the cooling caves helped our early ancestors survive both the winter and the summer. No one in Milway had air-conditioning back then. If there was an electric fan in the house, it was usually in your parents' room. Looking back, it's amazing to see how soft we've become, how dependent on things like air-conditioning we all are. Don't get me wrong. I'd never give up air-conditioning for the larger brains that the Cave Men had. They needed a bigger brain to survive, but it scares me a little to think how tiny the brains of twelve-year-olds in the future might be.

As the air around us changed color from dusk gray to tar black, and as the night conquered the entire area, we knew it was too late for anyone near by to yell, "Kick-the-Can?" Every time we got together on my front lawn to study the dark heavens and watch for shooting stars, especially in August, we'd end the evening by walking silently back to our houses meditating on all the topics we'd covered in our conversations. A simple, "See you tomorrow," was all we ever said to each other.

Years later, when Billy and I talked about recalling our summer youth, all he could remember was talking about wishing to find some cool cave so he could hide from the late summer's heat. Nothing slowed him down like the dog days of August. I remembered that concern also, but I also recalled conversations delving deep into the nature of space, other living beings, the enormous distances out there, and even how neat it would be to time-travel. Little did we know back then that we were time-traveling through the years, but doing it so slowly we never noticed the minutes and the hours speeding past us let alone full days, weeks, months, and even the years rocketing quickly away from us. Time means nothing to a twelve-year-old. The centuries from when our ancestors first walked out of Africa to cover all the earth, is but a mere blink of an eye for Time. His irresponsible brother, Luck, wanted to take all the credit for the success of our earliest migrating ancestors. Time said that He should talk to his cousin, Chance, before taking all the credit. Luck replied that Chance was always too busy keeping Her older and younger sisters from fighting with each other to ever be part of their fascinating conversations.

Those lazy warm summer evenings were only for speculating about things of which we knew very little. It was not a time for laying out fort building plans, making new rules for as yet unplanned games, or what else we might find in my grandfather's barn; no, it was only for philosophizing about what is, and what isn't. Most of the guys we hung around with remember the things we built, and the games we played. I just can't help thinking differently. Of all the things Billy and I did together, it is actually those empty nights filled with thousands of unanswered questions that I remember the most.

10

It hadn't been that long since my encounter with the tractor's right rear wheel, but my back didn't bother me much any more. When my mother asked, "How's your back feel? You've got to be careful on that bike."

I answered, "It's okay. I'm fine." I was certain that she was talking about when I told her I fell off my bike, never mentioning what had really happened with Jimmy and the tractor. But, it turns out, she was sore from reaching up and extending her arms for peaches, and thought I too might have some aching muscles.

Summer was in full swing. We played Robin Hood with our bow and arrows a lot of times, using the old barn as King John's castle. The more often we played, the more reckless we became, and all too often, fired arrows way too close to our companions.

Sammy Dugapol, whose father always joined my father and me to hunt on the first day of rabbit season in November, didn't play with us very much because he was older first of all, and secondly, he had to work at home much more than we ever did. However, he was with us one afternoon as we were making believe the king's men were chasing us, so we fired our arrows into all the wooden objects, including the fence at the back of the barn. Each hit stopped another of King John's wicked warriors, the same soldiers who humiliated the women, and harassed the old men. Standing on the cowshed's roof, I spotted Sammy running behind the barn across the open driveway toward the coal bins. Without thinking, I shot an arrow toward him. I didn't pull the bow back as tightly as when I shot at the wooden post. The arrow seems to float, not shriek, toward him. He ran right into it. It hit him in his leg, and he tumbled over onto the dirt. I froze thinking I might have killed him.

"Hey!" he screamed up to me as I stood on the barn's shop roof. "Are you crazy?" he continued with anger and fear in his voice.

The arrow didn't have enough force to drive into his flesh even though it broke the skin. It hit the side of his leg and dropped back out of the hole it made in his slacks. However, being older and wiser, Sammy decided he'd had enough of Robin Hood, and said he had to get home to pick eggs, something he was obligated to do nearly everyday. I slowly exhaled expelling all the fear I had into a faint cloud of mist. A ton of worry lifted from me. I told Billy that I also had chores to do, so I collected my spent arrows, including the one that hit Sammy in the leg, put my bow back into the yard shed, and went inside my house to wait for *Flash Gordon* to come on the TV. My youthful stupidity could have changed my entire life. Luck plays a very big part in determining our destinies. Luck, Time's dim-witted younger brother, would linger in our neighborhood, and be activated again on the following Saturday. I went off to deliver my newspapers after *Flash Gordon* was over and re-lived, in slow motion, the arrow leaving my bow, floating through the air, and then reaching its target, a human leg. To get it out of my mind, I'd have to keep very busy the next day or once again, I'd be haunted with how dumb I'd been. Few things made me more angry than when I did something really stupid.

*   *   *

As we concluded a late afternoon game of stickball behind Spitz's garage the following Friday, we all decided to play King Arthur, which was really Robin Hood but over at Billy's yard and chicken coops, instead of at my Grandfather's barn, where we'd planned to continue our knightly game the following day.

We had wooden swords and shields made with a wooden frame, and covered with old linoleum. Linoleum is a word every kid loves to say. Linoleum. We also had a few lances made from old broken rake handles. Ricky had a length of rusty old chain he'd swing against trees and fence poles that were usually viewed as being our enemy. We just made believe we had armor to put on before each battle. Billy's father had just begun to tear down one very old, long chicken coop, the one closest to his house. About a quarter of the building was lying on the ground with a long, thin section of the roof lying over all the two-by-fours, and a number of rusty iron frames where the chickens had laid their eggs. We had plenty of targets to use as the invading enemies. We'd drive the lances into the tar papered roof sections. Swing your sword at the parts of lumber still standing upright. Retreat, and launch arrows into the side of the untouched sections of the long coop. We fought like knights of old, and taking breaks only to collect our arrows, and then, continue to fight to save the kingdom from the always-evil invaders.

"Warriors to the far right," shouted Ricky.

"Archers ready," I said.

"Throw your lances before we have to sword fight," Billy screamed out.

"Fire," I said. Four arrows shot into the sky and fell against the chicken coop wall. Anthony's went the furthest. The enemy was stunned. Lances followed. "For King Arthur," we all shouted as we drew our swords, and ran toward the still-standing portion of the coop. What made it so exciting was the fact that we all believed, if just for those brief minutes, that we actually were Knights of the Round Table.

We'd swing our swords at imaginary warriors. We'd turn and smash our weapons at each other's swords making believe for a second or two that the other guy was an enemy attacking us. Then, we'd all swing back together and fight ghosts in the air until our arms were too tired to hold up our wooden swords. Medieval England had nothing over Milway. Our imaginations fired with the sights and sounds of merry old England. We knew Arthur would bestow honors on us when we returned, in our midnight's dreams, to the Round Table. I was a Knight of the realm among my fellow princes and lords. We couldn't believe how lucky we were to have Billy's father start to tear down the old chicken coop, the Black Knight's castle of despair. The sun never moved when we were entranced in our imaginary games; the day was as long as we wanted it to be. It was only when we slowed down that the day jumped ahead, and by late afternoon, just before dinner, when the sinking sun was by then falling into the western sky, did we interrupt our exhilarating crusade. Since it was already getting late in the afternoon, we all moved back to Billy's side yard, the side where you entered his house, not the far side where Tudor unseated Billy from his bike with his Lone Ranger cowboy rope trick.

Billy was still carrying his shield in an upright defensive position. Ricky had Billy's bow and arrows. Anthony lay back on the grass and listened to an owl that began to hoot from in the nearby woods. All the kids in Milway knew that owl. He sang to us every late afternoon, near dusk, and again every early morning when he seemed to know we were outside and able to hear him. After a moment of silence, Anthony asked if we all wanted to play Kick-the-Can after dinner. No one answered him. Again, there was just silence. I felt very accomplished for organizing a great day of playing Knights of the Round Table. I was just about to suggest we try to get some more guys for tomorrow's battles when Billy interrupted me.

"Hey, Ricky. Fire an arrow into my shield."

"Set it against that red maple," Ricky answered.

"No, I'll hold it. I want to see how far it'll push it back."

"Okay, hold the shield way out. Far away from you."

Billy stood up, held his left arm straight out holding the homemade shield. It was an inverted triangle. Two feet across the horizontal top, and both sides narrowing down to a point about thirty inches long on each side. It could have covered nearly all of him if he'd held it directly in front of him instead of holding it far out to his left side. Ricky was only about twelve or fifteen feet away. He slowly stood up, set his arrow, and drew it fully back. I didn't like the feeling I had of some strange force laughing down on us. I heard the snickering giggle floating in the soft, slow wind. I shivered in the heat. I instantly recalled my very soft shot into Sammy's leg not so long ago. Before I could shout to stop, Ricky released the bowstring, and fired one of Billy's own arrows at the shield.

The side door of the house opened as Billy's mother was just coming outside to call him in for dinner, and to also let us all know that it was time to head home. Instead of announcing dinner, she let out a bloodcurdling scream! Ricky's arrow, I could see from the other side of where Mrs. Strusser was standing on her step, had missed the shield by a quarter of an inch at most, and drove into Billy's outstretched bicep. It drove in at least a half an inch, maybe more. However, from where she was standing it looked like it had hit him right in the chest. She was certain that her son was about to drop over onto the ground. Maybe he was already dead, and his body was just waiting to drop. The scream made Billy drop the shield. Ricky dropped the bow and the quiver of arrows, and then he and Anthony ran off toward their home. I shouted, "It's in his arm! His arm. It's in his arm!"

It felt like it took an hour for her to run down the steps, and sprint to Billy. He was not shocked at all. He said, "Just my arm, Mom."

I knew it must have really hurt, maybe as much as the bee stings, but he didn't want her to scream again or shout at him.

She wasn't sure if she should pull out the arrow. We had, all three of us, seen too many Cowboy movies where they said to leave it in until you'd get to town, so Doc can take care of it. This time there was no hesitation. Billy yanked it out himself. He must not have been thinking of all the cowboy movies that were projecting through my mind, and most likely his mother's head. He just wanted the look on his mother's face to change. There wasn't even as much blood as a normal bloody nose. We'd all been hit, fallen, or had our noses bumped into enough times to know what a bloody mess a bloody nose can be. This was just a near-death incident that twelve-year-old boys never recognize as a near-death catastrophe. I slowly turned in a complete circle surveying the landscape to see if Chance or Her cousin, Luck, was watching us, but I saw nothing. Just the three of us standing peacefully on the green summer grass watching some tiny droplets of red blood drip slowly toward the earth. I'm sure every Knight in ancient England had experienced the same scene dozens of times.

Mrs. Strusser wrapped the dishtowel she had been carrying all around his arm, covering the wound where the blood dripped from the hole in his arm. "You'll need a tetanus shot, I'm sure," she said in a much calmer voice, "and maybe some stiches."

I said, " You'll be fine. I'll bet it doesn't hurt as much as a bee sting." I was speaking slowly, and with an almost adult tone in my voice. I wanted to help Billy and his mother relax a bit. She too, now seemed to know that her scream frightened Billy more than the arrow did. She, by then, was in complete motherly control.

The word stiches made Billy cringe. An arrow in his arm, all the blood, even his mother's scream didn't frighten him as much as thinking about getting stiches. I don't think it him hurt as much as when the rope caught him by the neck, and flipped him backwards off his bike and onto his driveway. Even what the wasps did to him at the start of summer had to have been more painful than a little arrow stuck in your arm. At twelve years old, you seldom thought about the consequence of your actions even though your parents tried to teach you that over and over again. Milway didn't seem like a dangerous place to me, but Billy, and definitely his mother, might have begun to have different thoughts about that.

After she went back to the house to get her car keys, Billy told me that the arrow didn't push his arm back much at all. He said that he should have had me fire the arrow. Ricky could throw farther than any of us, but that was his best and only skill. I repeated his words as I told him that I should have shot it because Ricky could throw a baseball the farthest, but he was never very good at shooting rats, using a BB gun, nor using a bow and arrow. I like to think if I had done it, I would have made him put the shield against the red maple tree and not hold it himself, but in all likelihood, I'd have just fired the arrow while he held it. But, I would have aimed at the outside edge, and not even at the center of the shield like Ricky had tried to do.

Since his mother had already left to get her car keys and we were alone, I told him I'd see him later, thinking that was better than saying tomorrow. I've never trusted tomorrows; I'd learned that with some people and odd situations, they have a strange way of never happening.

I don't think we really learned anything about being safe, thinking ahead, or applying the old adage, "better safe than sorry". On looking back we should have. If we did learn anything, it was accidental. At the time, we were still Knights that had to do battle. I was still Lord of the Land, and Prince of Milway. Billy did get a tetanus shot, but no stiches, only a butterfly bandage, and a lot of questions from the doctor about what he was playing, and who his friends were. I bet the next time a bunch of doctors got together to do whatever it is they do, he'd be the only doctor there who could talk about fixing an arrow wound in 1956 in the arm of a Knight from Milway.

I didn't see Billy again for two full days, and by then, we were already planning to spend a full night in my back yard camping out in my old tent. His upper arm was wrapped, but he seemed to be fine. Yesterdays disappear quickly. Today was fresh and new, and it demanded that we do something different. Sleeping outside on a summer's night should be mandatory for every boy everywhere. Yes, mandatory. I could see the bandage on his arm, but neither he nor

I said anything about it. Would Lancelot have brought it up? No. When you're twelve, everything is in the present: no past and no future, only right now. I wonder why that changes as we grow up?

*   *   *

I had to mow the lawn in our back yard anyway, so I mowed even farther back away from the house, all the way back to the big apple tree just ahead of the strawberry patch at the end of our property. The farmland behind us belonged to my grandfather. If Billy and I walked barefoot out of the tent during the night, the mowed grass would feel better on our feet. We had set up the tent dozens of times planning to sleep in it all night ever since school first let out for the summer, but something always changed our minds or interfered with our plans. This time everything seemed perfect. There was nearly a full moon, and the humidity was lower than it had been for a week. We had night snacks, ice tea in a thermos, one flashlight, and just outside the door flaps, we had an old coffee can half filled with kerosene, and a pinecone in it to serve as a wick. It would serve as a night-light until we fell asleep or it burned out. My uncle Popeye told me that he had learned how to do that in the Army.

I finished my paper route and ate dinner. Billy's mother put a clean bandage over his arrow wound. We met at the tent during that last half hour of visibility after the sun had already set. People call that short time-span dusk. The word dusk comes from an Old Saxon word for brown, *dosan*. It's not brown at all during that half hour when it's neither day nor night; it's gloomy, that's all, just gloomy. It's a time without shadows. Things like that bothered me for as long as I could remember. Those Anglo-Saxons stuck us with a weaker word. Very early in the morning, and just before night, your shadow sneaks off and hides. Maybe it spends time with Chance, Joy, or Sorrow, or maybe it simply sits beside that jester, Luck, listening to Him make future plans. When there is no shadow, Time too disappears, so your shadow must be frozen somewhere far away.

I put the pinecone in the kerosene-filled can, and set it on the ground in a spot where the lawn mower had cut out all the grass right down to the dirt. It was directly in front of our tent, only about five feet from the entrance. We lit the kerosene-soaked pinecone, and silently watched the flames begin to tango above the can. It gave plenty of light, and its scent also helped keep the mosquitoes away. We rolled out our sleeping bags, decided on letting the coffee can just burn itself out, closed the flaps and began munching on our camping-out snacks. We talked about building another fort before summer was over. I knew a spot in the nearby woods where there was a nearly full circle without any underbrush. Perfect. It would be in the strip of woods between the railroads tracks and Tuckahoe Road. It would be in a place that had no bees. We'd skip a raised tree platform, and just build some wooden enclosure. It might just be three circular huts instead of one singular big tepee.

We also talked about hayloft jumping like I did with my cousin Jimbo. I explained that before we ever jumped down into the hay again, we'd have to search carefully through the entire hay pile to make sure that nothing was left behind and hidden in the hay. We discussed the moon, and wondered if it were even possible to get there with a Flash Gordon rocket ship. The two of us decided that because there was no air on the moon, no one would ever be able to, or even want to step on the moon. We talked until the entire town was completely quiet, not a sound could be heard, not even the sound of a passing automobile. It was just when we decided to try to fall asleep, we saw it. The dark silhouette moved toward our tent with the bright moonlight behind it. Our kerosene lamp had burned itself out by then. Now, the only light came down from the sky. It was the face of the devil. Its profile showed large projections on top of its head. The coffee can flames were already out, and we had no weapons, nothing to fight it off. No one can ever prepare for a visit from Beelzebub.

When we turned on the flashlight, we heard it make a noise.

"Didn't sound like a devil," I whispered over to Billy.

"Didn't sound like a human either," he answered.

"Be careful."

"Move slowly," Billy added.

Then, the figure turned, and we saw its full outline. We hoped it didn't open the door flaps or crush into the tent. It looked like an enormous centaur at first, then it hee-hawed loudly, and then it hee-hawed once again without as much volume, so we opened only one tent flap, shined the flashlight on it, and saw that it was Billy's neighbor's donkey. We both quietly thanked God it wasn't the devil, but neither of us said anything out loud. The donkey froze like a deer in headlights. I turned off the flashlight, and it turned his head toward its home. The old man who rented the little house on Strusser's property kept it as a reminder of when he needed it to work the fields before tractors were so easily available. We seldom ever saw him, but we did see his donkey once in a while. Our devil's big ears stood upright. How it got out of its donkey shed, we couldn't imagine, but it quickly ignored us completely. The donkey slowly meandered back toward its own home, and quietly faded into the dark tree shadows, and once it was out of the moonlight, it disappeared.

"Sure scared me," I told Billy.

"Oh, I knew it wasn't no devil," he answered.

"Yea, sure," I replied. "Let's just go to sleep."

"I've never seen it roaming anywhere before," he said.

"You think anybody will believe this? I asked.

"No. Nobody will, except maybe Ricky," Billy suggested.

"With the moonlight behind its head, it sure looked like some kind of devil to me," I said.

Neither of us slept very well after that. Neither of us had ever seen the donkey away from its tiny barn. Both of us learned how quickly one's imagination could take over. Neither of our parents believed what had happened when we told them. You were just dreaming, they told us without explaining how we'd both had the same dream. Time's nitwit brother, Luck, must have kept the donkey from pushing in the sides of the small tent and stepping on us. Yep, we both thought, everyone should camp out and sleep in a tent at least once. Maybe once every summer until you're too old to remember ever being young.

11

The summer of 1956 was still in bloom, and on the following Monday, my two New York cousins, Eleanor and Carol, came down for a visit, as they said, to the farm country. They were two of the four girls my Uncle Packy and Aunt May had. Their oldest, and youngest sister couldn't come with them. They had lived in New York City all their lives and never went up the Empire State Building. They never saw the Statue of Liberty either. After I overheard them tell my brother Jimmy that when you lived near famous sites, you just take them for granted, and almost never have a reason to visit them. So I began to wonder what important things I had missed seeing in Milway. If you take things for granted, you may not be aware that they could be famous. Both their mother and their father were born in Ireland in the same area as my father's hometown. Their father was my father's younger brother. Carol and Eleanor's two other sisters couldn't come down because of work, and I only saw them one more time after that. It was at their father's viewing, or wake as they called it. That was my first real, but not last, experience with death, human death that is. My hound dog Elmer's death was buried away in the dark caverns of my mind, and never flowed back into the light along the tiny creeks of my memory.

When my parents and I walked into the viewing that was held for my uncle up in New York City, my father walked right up to my Aunt May, and whispered something to her, and then marched straight toward the coffin resting at the rear of the room. The chamber was full of people that I'd never seen before, and as my father walked toward the coffin to see his brother one last time, the congregation fell into a deathly silence. The lively conversations we'd heard as we walked into the funeral parlor instantly ceased. I didn't understand what was happening. The silence scared me. You could hear the older people slowly breathing. My father stopped and then knelt briefly before the coffin, then, as he stood back up and backed away I could see into the coffin. I could see how much the two brothers looked alike. I couldn't tell any difference from where I stood along side my mother. Most of the room full of guests had never seen our Milway family, and most of them had never met my father.

"Oh my God," said one older neighbor who was sitting in the first seat of the second row. "I thought Packy had risen, and came back in to see what was going on."

"I thought the same thing," said the lady across from him.

Then, I suddenly understood why everyone looked shocked. The man in the coffin looked almost exactly like my father. Packy, as he was called instead of Patrick, was my father John's nearly identical brother. No wonder everyone was stunned, I quietly thought to myself. They could almost be twins.

Well, it was a few years prior to our journey to my uncle's funeral that Carol and Eleanor visited Milway. They both smoked cigarettes, and drank coffee for breakfast. That's all, cigarettes and coffee. They went with my Uncle Mike to my grandfather's field on Millville Avenue, that was still a dirt road back then, and tried to help hoe in a corn field. They weren't very good at it. They didn't like the smell of the barn, but were happy to go with my parents to Vineland to shop one evening. They spent most of their time with my older brother Jimmy because they were almost the same age, but near the end of a week that grew ever hotter and hotter, Jimmy decided to take everyone to Kimble Bridge for a swim. It was a small road-bridge over the Kimble Creek between Milway and Milltown. It was our major swimming hole. There was a tree with a rope tied to it for swinging out, and then flying free to fling yourself out into the center of the small river where the water was the deepest. There was a very tiny beach near all the poison ivy that grew along one side of the stream, and just past where we'd usually swim, there were two small trees that had fallen across the water. We assumed that those smaller trees went down during the windy thunderstorm that went through the area the previous week. We usually had the place to ourselves except when the local East Vineland farm boys came over to cool off after working in their father's fields all day. We were usually there at noon or early afternoon, and we were long gone most of the time before any of the local kids got there. We mostly had the place to ourselves just as we would when Carol, Eleanor, Jimmy and I got there.

Because it had gotten hotter and hotter each day that week, I knew we'd have another thunderstorm soon. As we made plans for the swimming trip the next day, the wind picked up and blew like a hurricane. The sky completely darkened in less than twenty minutes. It began as a soft drizzle, but quickly morphed into a deluge so thick that you couldn't see through it. I used to love the sound of rain hitting the tin roof over our front porch, but this downpour played no music. It fell producing only one lone note, a deep kettledrum solo. Thunder drummed too, and lighting slashed across the sky. It poured like I've never seen it rain before. My mother worried about losing electricity, but all I could think about was how the river would be running faster, and would be deeper with all the run-off from the storm. Two inches of rain in a short period of time is quite a bit of water to contend with anywhere. I was a good athlete, but only average at best in swimming. I could never float on my back very well, and had to constantly work hard at swimming. The ocean's salt water helped some because salt water makes it easier to stay afloat, but the waves made it impossible for me to practice any long swims. I got nervous when my mother pulled a sweater over my head if it took too long, so drowning was always a constant fear, almost a phobia. But at twelve years old, you never let fear supersede peer pressure. You just jumped in when everyone else did, and hoped for the best.

Whenever I talked about my New York City cousins, I thought about the story of the country mouse, and his cousin, the city mouse. When the country mouse visited the city, he was nearly killed having never seen mousetraps, and all the dangers a city presented. I know the story could work both ways, and hoped my cousins wouldn't experience the tale in reverse. They were both about Jimmy's age, and I was just the tag-along kid.

They got up much later in the morning than I did. I'd already put a coat of car-wax on the fenders of my bike, saw Ricky and Billy in front of Spitz's gas station talking with Tudor, and went to tell them I couldn't play ball today because I had to go with my city cousins. I even had enough time to plant another iris that my mother had taken off from another cluster that she'd planted a few years ago. She called them flags. They were purple, and they smelled like a room full of mothers at a P.T.A. meeting. Every grownup lady I knew smelled like either iris or lilac. It was way too much for me. The only aroma I liked was the smell of freshly mowed grass. By the time I finished the planting and got back inside the house, Eleanor and Carol were waiting with their bathing suits on, and Jimmy was starting the pickup. I quickly changed, and off we went to Kimble Bridge to cool off from a heat wave that threatened both the newly planted zucchini, and any old people who had to work outside.

It was a ten-minute drive. Jimmy drove past the creek, made a U-turn, and parked facing home on the side where we'd venture down the forested hillside, and into the river. We left our towels and sneaks in the pickup so parking where we did meant not having to cross the blistering hot road with bare feet. The river on the other side of the road provided far less space for swimming, and it had no ropes to swing from either. The blistering road tar could burn the souls of your feet in seconds if you had to walk on it to cross the road barefooted. My brother may have been artistic, but I seldom knew him to be practical, so I was impressed that he had planned ahead when we parked the pickup. The two girls followed him down the road embankment, past the poison ivy, and onto the tiny sandy beach. I followed silently at a distance. I knew I'd be ignored the entire time we were there. I was just happy to get wet and cool off some during this blistering heat spell.

"Hey," he said, "let's move back toward the bridge and jump in from there. The water will push us right back to this beach."

"Okay," answered Carol who was quite adventurous for a city girl.

"You said it was a tiny creek, not a full river," Eleanor said.

"Usually is," Jimmy answered. "Remember all the rain we got last night. It's flowing twice as fast as it usually does. It's deeper too."

I'd been here lots of times, and I never saw the stream flowing this fast, nor ever saw the water so high up and overflowing onto its banks. The river flowed so quickly downstream that it would be nearly impossible to swim upstream against the current. The thunderstorm certainly had added an enormous amount of water to the creek. There were two or three other trees lying across the stream further past the sandy beach section of the wooded bank, trees that were not lying in the water the last time we were here. They must have been pushed over by yesterday's wind, I thought.

Jimmy jumped in first and let the rushing water carry him downstream to a small eddy where it was shallow enough so he could stand up. The two girls quickly followed, screaming as they jumped in like most girls do. I hesitated, but jumped in right after I saw them approaching Jimmy. I was sucked under, then bobbed up, and maybe because I was much smaller than the three much older teenagers, the water pushed me faster so I had to swim hard to reach the eddy where the other three had already ended up. The violently rushing water was exhilarating for the three older swimmers, but I viewed it as an ominous death trap. However, that first ride in the rapidly flowing water was more exciting than scary. I could wade back to the sandy bank. The other three were already making their way toward the tree with the rope hanging from a limb that grew out over the stream. They could use the rope to swing out, jump into the center of the river, and then let the water carry them across and down the creek to the safety of the sandbar where the shallow water was. You always do whatever your guests want to do, and you let them be the center of attention. I knew that was a family rule, maybe even a public law. I wasn't sure which, but it was a rule we always followed.

This was a day for my New York cousins to experience something they seldom or never got to do, so I didn't follow them immediately. Their only beach experience was visiting Coney Island and wading in the salty ocean. Carol, Eleanor, and Jimmy all had successful swings on the rope, and each of them rode the water down to the safety of the sandbar three times each before I even tried it once. After the blistering heat we had all week, I was content to sit on a small section of the moss-covered riverbank with my feet in the cooling water as it flowed by like the jet stream does in the winter sky.

"Try the rope again," Jimmy shouted.

The girls now felt obligated to make me a part of the activities so they also yelled to me that I should swing with them from the riverbank out into the center of the stream.

I left the comfort and safety of the riverbank, and returned to the tree with the rope hanging from it like a gallows. I'd seen enough episodes of *Gunsmoke* on television to understand foreshadowing, vultures circling over head, the rattle snake coiled in the rocks ahead of the approaching riders, and the swaying rope hanging on a gallows, all foreshadowing some catastrophe or some sinister event, but I ignored the premonitions. I went back as far as I could this time, and swung out to mid-steam before yelling, "Geronimo," and then let go. All the Milway boys shouted that famous Indian name before jumping anywhere. No reason. Whenever you jumped, you shouted it. We just did it without any explanation. "Geronimo!" Then jump.

Because I was farther out in the stream this time, I had a shorter ride to the safety of the eddy and the sandbar. I nearly went past it and had to grab one of the limbs of the newly fallen trees to pull myself out of the deeper water, and be able to stand up. I smiled with pride at my success as the three older swimmers were already heading back to the rope-tree. They each swung out on it and jumped two more times before I did it again. They were all having too much fun, and all three now ignored me completely. I didn't swing out as far when I did it the first time. I landed close to where I started, and caught a faster rush of water. I could feel myself being jetted along toward the trees lying across the surging water. The river pushed me up a bit, and I grabbed a big deep breath before it pulled me down again, and pushed me directly into the tree limbs. I wasn't more than six feet from the safety of the sandbar as I paddled upward toward the blue sky well above the surface of the water. That's when my head hit one of the limbs. My eyes were opened, and I could see where the water ended and the life-giving air began. I'd come up between a fork in a limb of the tree's outer branches. My head was only about six or seven inches from the oxygen I panicked for, but the forked limbs had caught each of my shoulders, and my head was between the two wooden arms holding me beneath the surface of the water. I felt panic. I knew my brother and cousins weren't paying any attention to me, and I would soon drown. Then, they'd be in big trouble, I thought. My face was staring at the safety of the oxygen-filled sunny sky, but the forked limbs prevented me from reaching it just inches away. What were the odds of my coming up in the exact spot that prohibited me from escaping the water? It had to be Luck's cousin, Chance, that had set the whole thing up, and was now toying with me.

I thought of my bike and paper route for some strange reason. Who'd deliver my papers that evening? I then thought about the fort Billy and I had built, the basketball court I'd raked clean and free of stones, and then saw Ricky playing Kick-the-Can. Again, I wondered who would deliver my newspapers that evening. The visions had a calming effect on me. With no logical planning, strictly out of instinct, I slowly put my two hands up against the two limbs, one on each side of my head, and pushed up against them. That action forced my body down below them even deeper, and farther away from escaping up to the air. I had to go down deeper, and then move to my left before I could rise upward and get out of the water. I moved ever so slightly to my left, and then I rose again. My face was out of the water. The forked-limbs I was stuck in were just below the water nearly touching my right shoulder. The current tried desperately to drag me into more limbs, and further downstream, but I used the left forked limb as a handle, and worked my way to the shallow water where I could stand up. I just stood still for a while forcing the spent, dead air out of my lungs, and then I took a deep, fresh, new breath of life. In less than a minute, the feeling of panic dissipated. I took two more long deep breaths, and then I very slowly walked back to the mossy riverbank. I could easily have drowned, but I wasn't dead. I was pretty sure I wasn't dead when I saw that idiot, Luck, behind my closed eyelids, scolding His cousin.

I took a few more rapid deep breaths, and then noticed my cousins trying to push Jimmy into the stream below the rope. They giggled. One screamed. He turned and dove in to swim across the torrent of water. Not one of of them had even noticed my dilemma. No one would have watched me die. I have been leery about swimming ever since that day at Kimble Bridge. Even if I was with a lot of people, in a river or at the beach, and they paid attention to me, I still took no excessive chances. I was the Prince of Milway, its trees, fields, barns and chicken coops. I was never the Captain of any body of water.

For the next half hour, I waded in and around the sandbar ignoring their shouts to use the rope again.

"Last call," Jimmy shouted to everyone. "It's about time we went home."

"Come on," yelled Eleanor, "we can swing together."

"I'm tired," I lied. I knew I'd been lucky by pushing myself deeper down to get out instead of just trying to squeeze through the two limbs holding me just inches from safety. I had no idea how I figured I had to go backwards first to be able to go forward and up to safety.

I knew I could have swung on the rope again and flowed right to the eddy and safety of the sandbar, but I could feel Time peering through the green overgrowth of the forest along the river saying don't fool around with Luck. He's an idiot, and He's very busy right now.

We were all cooled off and quite tired as we dried ourselves along side the pickup. We'd be home in about fifteen minutes, and then we'd all probably have an earlier dinner. I planned to do my paper route right away, still in my bathing suit, and then change into my long pants for stickball hoping to have enough daylight to get at least one quick three-inning game in with the guys. I didn't want to go to sleep too early. I knew what I'd dream about, and I didn't want to say anything about nearly drowning to anybody. The more hours I was away from that frightening event, the more scared I seemed to be as I kept thinking about being so close to a mouth full of fresh air and not being able to reach it. I would need a revitalizing new sunrise, and an entirely different activity to help me to get over it.

*   *   *

My cousins were heading home to New York City the next morning, so I decided to skip the stickball game and just hang around the house to listen to them tell stories about their New York Riverdale neighborhood, their friends, and Aunt May and Uncle Packy. Their entire world consisted of just a square block or two while I had the entire planet from horizon to horizon filled with barns and castles, fields and enchanted forests, and railroad tracks, and all the trains that supplied hundreds of visitors everyday to study my creations and peak in on my adventures to help them reflect about a time when they too, were princes, dukes, lords, and knights in their own youthful realms.

The next day was as hot as it had been before the reviving

rainstorm with its flood of refreshing waters, and its dangerous gushing streams. Carol and Eleanor left with fun-filled memories. I, on the other had, had a recollection I'd never forget. It would be sweltering when they got back to the city, but every thought of Kimble Bridge, and the rope tree that was used to help provide some refreshment and relief, was gone from my mind. I had no refreshing memories left, just thoughts about the excessive summer heat.

It was blistering hot the next few days. We all had to skip Kick-the-Can, stick or baseball, even riding our bikes very far. Tudor and Anthony had their own limited chores to do, and after they quickly finished them, they both just sat near the big fan in Spitz's garage. All the other kids in town seemed to disappear. I told Ricky and Billy that I had read a small book about the Cavemen and how they first used fire. I said that the caves kept them warm in winter and cool in summer.

"A cave!" shouted Billy. "That's what we need."

"I never heard of a cave anywhere in Milway," Ricky answered.

"We'll just have to find some place to make our own cave," I said. "I'll start looking, but for now, let's explore what's left of that chicken coop your father's tearing down," I said to Billy.

"It's only half done. The walls and roof are lying on the cement floor. We can get to the top part of what's left because a big part of the old roof is leaning against the side wall," he replied. "An easy climb up. We can play mountain climbers. No, let's be Indian scouts." Anticipation of any new activity can over-power the lethargy caused by even excessive heat.

We walked from my front yard over to Billy's house, and then up to the first chicken coop that Billy's father had ever built. The first half of the long, thin, old building laid scattered on the ground like a bomb had hit it. We could have played Army and fought Nazis in the rubble, but being Indian scouts was fine on a day when desert-like heat forced each of us to move about more slowly than usual. This new day provided a new life to see and experience some new adventures; just like getting out of those forked tree limbs in the water at Kimble Bridge had done for me. I didn't want to rush anything. A snail's pace is perfect for boiling summer days.

Once we decided upon being Indians, we slowed to a crawl. We crept from bush to bush and slowly approached the lumber, broken window frames, large portions of the side walls, and ten to twenty square feet of plywood roofing still covered with faded black tar paper. We knew the cavalry was hunting for us. The Blue Coats would take us to their white-man prisons if we got caught, so we moved extra carefully, to be quiet and hidden through nail-filled two-by-fours, broken window panes of scattered sharp glass, and sections of the tin roost where dozens of hens would sit on them, and lay their eggs.

The noontime siren went off at the fire hall, and we knew we had to head home for lunch. Ricky suggested we bring back our bows and arrows after we ate. I'd had enough of bow and arrows at Billy's house and said that we can all bring back our cap pistols, and we'd change sides from being Indians to being cavalry soldiers. After lunch we'd be the army hunting for Geronimo, and his tribe, instead of being Indians hiding from the army.

"Good idea," Ricky said.

"Yea," said Billy. "The Bluecoats won after all, and we should be on the winning side."

"Okay," I said to them both. "It's cap pistols when we get back."

They agreed, and we each headed home. We were the only three living things moving about in the blistering summer heat. My brother Jimmy, Sammy, all the older guys around Milway, and even all the adults, were nowhere to be seen outside in the heat of day. Not a single person visited the Post Office while I ate lunch. We had Milway all to ourselves.

Peter Pan peanut butter, and Welch's grape jelly never tasted better. I had a really big glass of ice tea with it. Two full glasses. We learned to be independent by making up our own games. Our parents never knew where we were, but expected us to be responsible by getting home on time for both lunch and dinner. They got used to us being away at school most of the year, and they knew that our lives and schedules were structured, so during summer, when we were outside, it must have felt to them that we were safe, just having fun, learning, and growing up all too quickly in their opinions. I, and all my friends never noticed that we were growing at all. We were exactly the same as we'd always been… and always would be. Being in elementary school, or playing at home should have really been about the same. The main difference, I believed at that period of my life, was that all the extra hours of summer daylight provided us with endless additional time that just doesn't exist at any other season of the year. *Carpe Diem.*

After lunch, I had garden tools to clean and put away. I had to start trimming the hedgerow that ran along the side of our backyard. If you cut just ten feet a day, you could have it all done in a week. I kept a watch toward Ricky's house to see when he would return to the Indian encampment in Billy's side yard at the chicken coop demolition site. All three of us had fresh new sneaks enabling us to run faster, and jump higher, but we'd all wait for a cooler day to test them with Mercury's wings. Today, we'd crawl; tip-toe among the fallen lumber, and jump downward letting the earth pull us effortlessly toward it, and not jump upward where we'd have to exert additional energy to rise above it. We knew that gravity always won, and it was much too hot to fight it today.

As I put the garden rake and hoe back into our shed, I spotted Ricky leaving his house and firing his cap gun. I grabbed my cap pistol, and headed toward Billy's.

The sun was in the western side of the sky by then, and all the shadows were longer, but it still was a furnace of a day.

Billy was already at the coop when Ricky and I arrived only to hear his mother shout out, "Be careful around that junk."

No one answered her. Billy gave her a wave with his hand, but no verbal response to her instruction about being careful. It had been a very full week with my New York cousins visiting, my close call in the river, and with the excessive heat, I could see that even my friends were, like me, too tired to even respond to our mother's commands.

I was glad to have had my New York cousins visit us. I knew so few of my father's side of our family. I spent endless hours with my mother's mother and father, and all her brothers and sisters. It was good to learn that there are lots of things out there that we need to learn about.

As we began to climb around the wreckage of the old chicken coop, I told Ricky and Billy about how my New York cousins smoked and drank so much coffee. I told them that they didn't know very much about farming, but they were willing to try anything. I concluded my report by saying we went swimming down at Kimble Bridge, swung from the rope hanging from the tree, and that the water was really much deeper than I'd ever seen it, but said nothing about how Chance was also there with her sister, Sorrow. I did tell them how Time made the afternoon stand still and there were a few seconds while in the water that seemed like a lifetime.

11-A

We were free to grow up. If freedom really is just another word for having nothing to worry about, then I was absolutely worry-free. The freedom of youth may be the most valuable thing in the world. Freedom is priceless. Sadly, you're seldom aware of just how rich you are when you're that young. I had nothing except the freedom of endless days and nights to contemplate everything that was around me. I lived in Milway, the most unique place on the earth, and I had the entire world at my feet. I was free to live through a timeless vacation from the ridged schedules of school. The summer of 1956 must have been the longest time span ever recorded in history. About twenty-five years later, I tried to let my own children have unlimited freedom to grow and explore, and learn personal responsibility; I had learned from my mother and father that I would be successful as a parent if my own children could survive without me. Sadly, they never had a summer as long as I did, and I doubt their children will ever have a summer as long, and as carefree as the summer of 1956. No, that earth no longer circles that same sun. The year is shorter and we measure time differently now. In fact, that earth is somewhere far off, yes, far away, in a different distant universe from where it was when I was twelve. Only the Big Dipper remains the same.

I think Time sneers at us a lot more today as He spies on modern twelve-year-olds. He must tire of their daily routines. Few, if any, young kids try to flatten pennies on a railroad track, or get the opportunity to drop glass bombs. I wonder what adventures our children are missing when all they have are community-sponsored playgrounds with soft rubberized surfaces beneath their store-bought plastic swings.

If the surface of the earth was too hot, we'd find a way to get below it. If too much snow brought everything to a standstill, we'd put it to use, and build an enclosure with it. Empty deserted buildings easily became our playgrounds. No one ever spent any money to buy a swing if you could find a discarded old tire and some rope. Yes, Time's knucklehead brother infrequently lingers in our area now, so you always have to be thinking, always trying to be smart, especially on really hot days when He's nowhere in sight. Yes, Luck can be a knucklehead, an idiot, a numbskull, but when we grew up we accepted everyone, and it sure paid off having Him hang around with us once in a while.

There was a lot of pain inflected upon my best pal, Billy, but he seldom, if ever, talked about what he had to put up with as a member of our Milway gang. I had no idea what he ever did to annoy Luck, but even when he grew older, they seemed to be at odds with one another. He had more car accidents than anyone I know.

The only thing Billy ever mentioned when we gave up our youthful freedom, and became prisoners of our adult lives, was the summer evenings when we'd lie on the grass in my front yard, and question each other about all the stars we could see. There was no pain in those conversations, only the joy of living with wonder. The sights, and sounds, and smells of Milway were imbedded into all the back gravel-filled roads of our brains. Once we had a word for something new, we could memorize it no matter how complex it was. Then, we'd think using that new word. Sights, sounds, and smells all had their differences, and at the same time, because they were all a part of Milway, they all had their similarities.

We always reclined in the exact same spot on my small front lawn as the sun fell into the western woods, and the stars began to appear at first in the eastern sky, and then all across the heavens. The grass seemed softer between the spruce tree and the road. It was our viewing spot to look for the twenty or thirty meteors that burned themselves into dust, as they became shooting stars soaring across the August sky. Space rocks from the *Perseids* or the *Geminids* have been providing a fireworks display ever since the first men looked upward into the night sky. Billy and I did the exact same thing. Little has changed since we first walked upright and stared at the night sky instead of looking down at our feet and the grassy earth we stood upon. Billy and I often wondered if any of those fiery burning rocks came from Superman's home planet. We questioned if any of the shooting stars we saw could ever hit Flash Gordon as he journeyed through space. We learned how to be concerned about a lot of things. Chance's younger sister, Joy, sat along side of us many times, and She smiled when we said amusing things. She knew we'd be forced to spend time with her older sister, Sorrow, as we aged, but like Billy and I, she lived in the moment.

My mother liked reading magazines more than watching television. My father always had a book open. He was the only kid in his hometown back in Ireland to ever complete eighth grade. Their influence and example helped make me an avid reader. Billy didn't care for reading too much. Together we made a great team; he asked questions, and I provided some possible answers.

Every night we added a new star to our mental map of the universe. We knew that near the end of the summer, the sky would be filled with shooting stars like it always was, and we had to be quick to see them, and record them into our memories. Wonder was everywhere. We were twelve years old, and we were living through the longest summer the world had ever known.

12

Pop! Pop! Pop! The sound of Ricky's cap pistol echoed off the side of what remained standing of the old chicken coop. Billy and I huddled in a cluster of broken two-by-fours, bent, rusty nails, and sections of the ancient tin roost. All the sections of the original chicken coop were scattered about. The tin was too hot to touch or pick up. Ricky joined our huddle, and after firing our cap pistols in unison for a while, he suggested we get up on the roof.

"Be smarter than the Indians," he said. "We have to have the high point looking down. We can ambush them from above."

"Good idea," said Billy. He started immediately to climb up sections of the torn-down chicken coop trying to reach a part of the still remaining roof on the untouched section of the building.

"Don't let them see us," I said making believe that we were surrounded by Indians who had been forced to fight back after being chased off their ancestral lands. We usually liked being Indians better than solders, but bows and arrows were out of the question anywhere near Billy's house for the foreseeable future.

"Watch the glass," said Billy. "It's sharp, and there's broken pieces everywhere."

"The nails will rip your pants if you're not careful," I said.

"Yes, watch out for nails," Billy repeated.

"Hey, you can feel a little air moving up here," Ricky announced after being the first to get on the coop's roof.

"Much better," Billy said, when he joined Ricky, and felt the slight breath of moving air.

"Let's scout the area," I told them after I too reached the top. "We can see all around from up here."

There was at least another hundred feet of chicken coop still standing that would soon be demolished. It ran parallel to the road between Billy's property and Spitz's gas station. From up there we could survey Billy's father's entire farm, and see his other two chicken coops. We could see Ricky's property, and the top of the barn and the basketball court on the back wall of the building behind the row of hedges between the coal bins, and Billy's side yard. The door was open to the potato house at my grandfather's. It was still filled with empty crates waiting for autumn's harvest. The chicken coop roof was slanted from north to south, and covered with a tarpaper that had white sand on it. The white sand reflects the sun's heat better than normal black tarpaper, and it would help keep the chickens inside the coop a little cooler. Of course there were no more chickens in this particular coop. The removal of this coop, and soon afterwards the destruction of my grandfather's barn, were the first signs of any major change in the Milway we had always known.

Our parents told us that staying the same is abnormal, and change is really the normal way of life, but none of us liked that idea, and we all sensed that old Time was behind the plot to upset our routines. We all knew that none of our parents should really be blamed for anything that Time was changing.

We walked up to the highest edge of the roof and from there, we could see the Kupenski Bar, and the field where my brother almost did me in with the tractor and disk. I could see where the man would drop off today's newspapers for me to deliver a little later on. We could see the railroad crossing, but no other section of the rails because they were below the dirt bank running along side the pepper field. The peppers had been harvested by then, and the field was taken over by the wild grasses and historic weeds until next spring's plowing, disking, and planting of some other crop. As soon as it thickened with grass, it would become our autumn football field when chilled air once again blew across our teary eyelids. We would have welcomed any cooler air if it didn't contain the obligation of returning to the confines of a classroom. Yes, we did have a strong desire for some cooler air, but no wish for autumn air could overpower our desire to maintain the freedom of summer. Time moved slowly, and so did we as we played moving back and forth along the rooftop of the remaining section of the old chicken coop.

"Here they come," Ricky said, pretending that a car traveling by was a raiding party of Indians.

"Get down," I said.

" That's not the main group," said Billy, "only a scouting party." He returned his cap pistol to his holster.

"Hey, Johnny," Billy said. "There's the newspaper man dropping off your bundle over at the bar. Look."

"I better go," I responded.

"Tomorrow. Right back up here," Ricky said. "Okay?"

"Okay," we both answered.

All three of us walked to the lower edge of the roof and jumped simultaneously down toward a large piece of a sidewall section lying over a pile of two-by-fours.

"If it's this hot tomorrow," Billy noted, "we'd better find a cave to stay in."

Those words stuck in my mind as I stopped by my house to tell my mother I was going for the papers. I picked up my bike, and then noticed the drainage ditch along the road nearest my house. The field ran at least four, maybe five feet high up above the ditch. Too bad there's no cave entrance there, I thought to myself.

*   *   *

Riding around Milway delivering my papers that late summer afternoon turned out to really be a scouting mission. Not for cowboys and Indians; no I was looking for spots where we could dig our own cave. "Make it yourself, or do without it," my father always said. He learned that quote from his father. I knew there were no real caves anywhere in all of South Jersey, but I knew our cellar, with the sleeping Mason jars of golden peaches was the coolest area in our house. Billy's house had a cellar with two different levels, and the lower one was cooler than the upper level. Ricky and Anthony's cellar with its sleeping wine barrel was the coolest spot around because it was deeper than either Billy's first cellar, or any part of my cellar. Yep, I thought, we could ditch in from the drainage bank a few feet, and then dig deeper for a room large enough for the guys to crawl into so we could all avoid each afternoon's Sahara's heat.

I thought about being in the cave we'd dig, and then have the ceiling collapsing in on us. What could we use as supports? I also tried to figure how deep we'd have to dig. When I flung the paper off at Ricky's front steps, and began my sprinting escape from their never-tiring hateful dog, I spotted the staves of an old wine barrel. Wood, I thought. We'd make our own cave roof, and use the dirt we dug out of the orange gravelly ground to cover the wood we'd put across the top opening. All the dirt we'd dig out would be more than enough to cool our cave. It would all depend on just how deep we wanted to dig. The deeper we went down, the more dirt we'd have to cover the roof and the cooler it would be. After we shot or captured Geronimo tomorrow at Billy's chicken coop, I'd layout the mechanical engineering for the roof sections, and then plan the civil engineering for our next and biggest project anyone in Milway had ever done. The cavern would be as big or even bigger than last winter's igloo.

I finished delivering my papers, checked to see if the Phillies, or even the A's whom I'd abandoned as my favorite team, were moving up the standings. I recalled my brother had said the Phillies were in the 1950 World Series; I couldn't remember that. I rushed through dinner asking my father how a roof stays up with all its weight. He explained that rafters slanted downward to move the weight toward the sidewalls. That was the key. He also said that in ancient churches, they had flying buttresses to help support heavy roofs, but that, I knew, was for above ground structures. I was sure I could slant the roof over our cave's big central room, and then we'd have solved the problem of having a cool place to escape the fire-hot days that we knew were still ahead of us.

Early that evening, right after dinner, I looked for another roll of caps, as we called them, the little rolls of paper with tiny explosive spots that went through our cap pistols. I put a new roll into my gun, and went to wash-up early so I could stay awake to see *The $64,000 Question* on CBS. How could some of those people know so much, I wondered. I wanted to know more too. Maybe in time I might be on that show. I knew my mom could use all the money that I might win.

*   *   *

I was at Billy's house before he'd finished breakfast. His older sister, Joanne, was planning to go to the beach with her friends. His younger sister, Barbara, was just big enough to be out of her highchair. Being in the middle may have given Billy less attention, but he got far more freedom by being left alone. We left his kitchen together and headed back to pick up where we left off the afternoon before. We were back up on the roof before Ricky even got there. I thought the Indians might even beat him today.

When he did arrive, I heard, "Hey, it's Geronimo," from Billy, referring to Ricky as he saw him stepping carefully through the broken pieces of two-by-fours, over bent tin and rusty nails, to climb up and join us where we looked down upon the discarded lumber.

He safely climbed up to where we stood on the lower part of the still morning-cooled roof. We ran back along the roof, made believe we spotted the entire tribe, and commenced firing our cap pistols without any consideration of being out-numbered by over a hundred to one. Pop after pop was sounded. "Bang," we added vocally every once in a while. "Bang. Bang."

"We got 'em scared!" Billy exclaimed.

"Keep firing, " I added.

"Let's jump down and chase them," Ricky said, as he ran to the end of the coop overlooking all the broken demolition exactly where we had jumped down the day before. He started to go, then turned and waited for the two of us to join him so we could all fling into the air together, land, and then run off firing our pistols at the fleeing frightened Indians.

Without any hesitation, as soon as we reached Ricky, we all jumped down onto the discarded lumber. Thump, thump, thump, we all heard as the three of us landed. Ricky landed farther forward than Billy and I did, and then he jumped toward the grass off the old concrete floor of the coop. I safely stepped over some tin and nails, and then jumped to the grass. Billy just stood there. He didn't move an inch. Like a marble statue, he was frozen in the spot where he landed. Ricky and I both looked back at him as we waited for him to join us in chasing Geronimo. He simply stood perfectly still in the same spot where he landed. He stared at his house as all the color faded from his face. "Ahhh," he said first, and then he let out a blood-curdling scream! He had landed on not one, but two upright sixteen-penny nails sticking upright through the tarpaper-covered plywood. All three of us were wearing our well worn-summer sneakers. Ricky's and my sneakers simply had green grass stains on them. Billy's sneakers started to have red bloodstains appear near the bottoms of each one. He had nailed himself right onto the wood. One nail impaled up into each foot. What were the odds? I surveyed the entire horizon for Time's goofy brother, but no one else was around.

Ricky started to wisely head home fearing Billy's mother, but I called to him to run and get his mother. She's had a lot of experience fixing his incredible injuries so I knew only she could solve this catastrophe. I jumped back toward Billy, stepping only on open parts of the old concrete floor, and asked if he could lift either foot. Tears flowed steadily from each eye as he cried out words that were hard to understand, "No, I'm stuck here," but he bravely tried anyway. His right foot pulled up off one of the rusty nails. He set it down on an open spot of solid concrete, sniffed, wiped the water off his face, and looked up to see his mother coming out of the house even before Ricky got there. She'd heard her son's scream. Ricky stopped in his tracks, and spun around to return to us. She rushed even faster to get to us. She got there just in time to take his extended hand just as he put all his weight on the freed bloody foot, and yanked his left foot up, and off the other rusty nail. It wasn't easy to lift his feet, but using every bit of his strength, he'd freed himself.

"Oh my God,"she said, over and over again."Oh my God."

Billy stepped to the grass by walking only on his toes. He sat down while she unlaced and took off his sneaks. Both socks were bloody red.

"Stay right where you are," she told him. "I'll bring the car over here. You need a doctor."

That was a sentence that we'd heard her say many, many times before. "You need a doctor." If his socks hadn't been so bloody, we might have laughed when we heard her say it. There was nothing funny about seeing your best friend being impaled. He nailed himself right to the frame of an old part of the roof that now lay on the ground. We shuddered thinking about the pain it must have caused.

She went for the car. Ricky headed home, and I just stood there looking at his feet until his mother came back. While waiting I said over and over again, "What are the odds? What are the odds?" We've all stepped on a nail, but if we had shoes on, it just broke some skin. With sneaks, it went deeper, but peroxide and iodine usually took care of our smaller wounds for us. We walked softly for a day or two, that's all. I was more shocked at the improbability of it all than at the sight of all the blood. Billy's shock had lessened, and he said he didn't want to go to the doctor, but his mother saw how rusty the nails were, and she didn't know if his recent tetanus shot from the arrow incident was still good enough.

I helped him up and into the passenger side of her car after she wrapped his feet with two dishtowels held on with some tape she'd brought from the kitchen where she'd gotten her car keys. The tears stopped flowing, and nothing remained but the look a dog has when you hold up an empty hand for him, an anxious, eerie, and bewildering look. No bone. No reward. Just disappointment. He looked like an elusive butterfly that no one, not even his mother, could touch. Nobody had ever looked sadder or more depressed. Chance was there when the three of us jumped, but Her cousin, Luck, absent minded as always, was nowhere to be found. He seemed to be avoiding Billy's property quite often that summer. None of us ever found out why.

Billy was back from the doctor's before lunchtime, but I didn't go over to see him. I felt better after I saw his mother's car head into their driveway. I didn't go visit him. I didn't see him at all until long after he was able to come visit me. I knew his mother's two major wishes were for summer to get over with, and secondly, to not see any of us playing together again for a while, a long while. I knew that Time's idiotic, imbecile brother, Luck, had completely skipped over Milway that day.

We couldn't play any games across the street from Billy's because we all knew that we wouldn't want him to see us all running, laughing, or calling out, "You're It!" while he had to sit inside and keep both his feet raised. Ricky rode his bike over to my house later that afternoon, and said that he'd ride with me while I was doing my paper route. I loved the company, but mostly it meant he'd take his own paper home when we were finished delivering the news to the people of Milway, who actually didn't care about anything else in the world besides the price of eggs, and tomorrow's weather.

He'd take the last paper home himself, and I could happily avoid the daily conflict with his family's dog.

We didn't say much to each other as we biked along my regular paper route. I'm pretty sure he was thinking the same thing as I was thinking: what are the odds? A million to one? Stepping on a nail was not uncommon in the Milway of my youth, but nailing yourself to a piece of old wood with two vindictive nails facing upward, just waiting like a coiled rattle snake for a victim to land on both of them at once was simply inconceivable. What were the odds?

No one had seen or sensed that Luck was anywhere around for some time now, so none of us dared do anything risky. We'd have to either see Billy playing back with our pack again, or wait for some confirmation that dopey old Luck had returned to our summer kingdom.

13

Ricky, Anthony, and their younger brothers Philip and Jo-Jo, came over first thing the next day to help me begin digging. I had already picked a spot along the ditch between the road and the far end of the old pepper field where very few large bushes were growing. That meant we'd have fewer roots to dig through. Trying to push a shovel through roots will always slow down any digging as I had learned the year before when my mother wanted me to plant a maple tree in our back yard. Jimmy, my father, and I started in three different places before we found a spot where we could dig a hole large enough to accept the maple tree root-ball. The first two locations were filled with way too many old roots from trees that had been gone for years, maybe even decades. There was nothing left of those old trees above ground now, but the ancient roots still hadn't decayed. Picking the right location for digging is the same as finding a perfect spot to build a home, or start a business. It's all location, as realtors always say.

I had only two shovels. Anthony sent Phil home to get another one. Ricky and I began to dig in a straight-line from the embankment toward the railroad tracks that were about fifty yards away. We were facing Mrs. Malatina's Grocery Store. Each of us, with a nickel in our pockets, could take a break whenever we wanted, and make a visit across the tracks to see her and get a chocolate fudge icicle. We did it a number of times during the days we were on this project, and it took a few times to learn that chocolate left you still thirsty, and that a lemon icicle was much better on really hot days. We made fewer and fewer trips over to my back yard to get a drink from the garden hose, because whenever we all went together for a drink, who ever was last would almost always spray all the others after he took his turn to drink. Knowledge can be obtained anywhere if you're open to learning. We all learned that lemon makes you less thirsty than chocolate, and we also learned that whomever is last to use a garden hose simply cannot help but try to spray everyone else. We always got sprayed. By the time we walked back to our man-made cave entrance, only a football field away, we were usually quite dry from the garden hose spraying. However, we all quickly began to sweat profusely once again as we labored beneath the late summer sun that had increased its wrath because it knew the season was nearing its end. No one could have paid us enough to do what we were enthusiastically doing for nothing.

The side section of the field we were uprooting hadn't been planted for a few years, and it was entirely overgrown with thick wild weeds. A meadowlark shot into the air when we first put our shovels into the grassy earth. They're beautiful black and white birds that nest on the ground. They used to be found all over Milway, but not anymore. I no longer ever see them. Gone also are the quail, whippoorwills, and barn-sparrows. As you approached a meadowlark nest, the mother would scurry away from it staying on the ground, and making believe her wing was hurt or broken as she ran just fast enough to keep ahead of you. Her acting would draw away any dog, or cat, or any predator, and trick them into thinking she was an easy catch. They would, sometimes, lead me all the way to the railroad tracks leaving her nest in relative safety. Then she'd fly off in a direction away from the nest, land, look back, and be sure you weren't returning toward her nesting area. If you were, she'd fly back, and repeat her injury scenario. Even today I'm amazed at how smart most animals are compared to most of the city-raised kids I met when I was in college.

The field is still there, and it looks exactly the same, but without any meadowlarks. It's overgrown entirely with strange grass and wild weeds now, but my cousin, Gary, who helped us get cardboard boxes for our igloo during the prior winter, mows it every once in a while so it looks very much like it did in 1956 when we were carving out the town's first and only subterranean cave.

Anthony was older and bigger than Ricky, but Ricky worked much harder. Ricky dug with Philip at what would be the center of the cave while Anthony dug a small ditch of nearly eight feet long and six or seven inches deep. I followed along where he dug, and squared-off the edges. We wanted the entrance tunnel to have straight vertical sides. Anthony had only dug for about half an hour before saying, "Hey, I better go get those barrel staves you said you wanted. Come on Phil. You too, Jo-Jo. Help me carry them back here."

Philip said, "I'll go and get my wagon. They might all fit in it." They didn't. It took two trips to get them all to the cave entrance. We then used a single barrel stave as a measuring stick to see how wide we'd make the tunnel entrance.

We quickly learned that we had to throw the dirt farther away from the edge of our ditch because some of it always fell back into where we were digging, and if it were left too close to the edge of the ditch, we'd have no place to set down the edges of the wooden ceiling we planned to build over the cave area. Everything's a learning experience when you're twelve.

"Billy coming over?" asked Anthony.

"I don't think so," I responded. "Both of his feet were swollen, but his mother told my mother that the doctor said no ligaments were hurt, no nerve damage, and he didn't need another tetanus shot since he had already gotten one this year."

"What are the odds?" Ricky repeated my words from our shock at seeing him nailing himself down to the old plywood siding. The nails that got him were the only two nails sticking up through the old rotten wood. All the other nails faced downward and could never have hurt anybody.

The doctor had to clean out the wounds because the nails were rusty and quite dirty, but Billy would be walking and running as soon as the swelling went down. He would, however, need new sneaks, and unless we did extra biking, extra evenings playing Kick-the-Can, extra time at baseball, basketball, and barn climbing, his new sneaks would never be worn out enough by the time school started to get a fresh new pair to use after school and during our autumn weekend adventures. He'd be the only guy not able to smell the newness that fresh sneaks provide as soon as we all got home from school for at least the first full week of when we once again had to relinquish our freedom and conform to the regulations of the adult world. Adults always talk about the smell of a new car. That's because their brains crave the pleasure they once got from the smell of a new pair of sneaks. All of our longest-lived memories first entered our heads through our noses. But that concern was a million miles away, and centuries into the future. Right now, to save ourselves from the hottest August we'd ever known, we needed a subterranean cave, a clandestine escape from the revengeful sun that Time was pushing more and more into the southern sky.

*   *   *

When I returned to our work site after quickly eating a hardboiled egg sandwich for lunch, only Ricky came back to join me. We dug for over two more hours before we couldn't stand the direct sunshine any longer. We had our entrance down to just over six inches deep, about three feet wide, and close to eight feet long. Tomorrow, we'd dig it deep enough to maybe set the roof of barrel staves over it, and hopefully have enough time to begin covering it with dirt. We'd also try to remove the grass-root level of soil around the entire circle we'd planned to be the main part of our cave. Digging through even short grass roots made it harder and slower to dig than into just pain old dirt. Forcing your shovel down through grassy roots is always the hardest part of digging. Once you got down to stony gravel, sand, even clay, you'd be able to dig faster, and with less effort. The part of the field we were in wasn't as tractor-packed as much as farther into the field where the soil would have been rock hard. We had been very fortunate. I had selected an easier digging location; maybe the best spot in all of Milway. Although it was hard work, we had an ideal spot for a cave.

Ricky said he thought he might be able to find some old tarpaper that we could put over the wood roof before we covered it with dirt. Our cave roof, with tarpaper under the dirt, would make it almost waterproof, even better than we'd hoped for, we both thought. It would keep the wood from rotting too, and maybe the cave would last forever.

After I delivered my afternoon papers, I searched the garage, the barn, and shop areas for tarpaper. I found half a pack of old roofing shingles that would help, two old root beer soda signs about two feet high and three feet long, most likely from Kupenski's Bar, and some torn canvas my uncles used to cover floors when painting interior walls or ceilings. The two signs together would cover twelve square feet of our cave's ceiling. My uncle Foxy was the painter in the family. He told me that once he finished a paint job near Atlantic City for a woman who wanted two coats of paint on her walls. He told her he used the special double-coating brush; one coat went on when he went to the left, and the other was applied when he went back to the right. Uncle Foxy was a con artist. He got paid for putting on two coats of paint at that job. She was happy. He saved time and money. Growing up with conniving uncles taught me to be very leery when dealing with people selling you stuff, or when workmen, who came to repair things, made it sound too easy. You seldom get all that you pay for, and you never know how you've been scammed. Even as kids, we couldn't believe that the woman bought Uncle Foxy's explanation.

The next afternoon Billy rode his bike over to see how we were making out with the cave. The only information he had gotten so far was from his mother who, in turn, had gotten her cave update from my mother. She referred to it as a pit. I'm certain she had an oubliette image in her mind. Billy was surprised to see that the entrance was not a small opening dungeon-like depression. He couldn't dig or even stand for a long time, but peddling a bike didn't seem to hurt his feet. It was great seeing him outside, and back with our group, for what seemed like ages to all of us since we'd last seen him.

"Is that the entrance, or part of the main cave?" he asked. He was still trying to erase the image that his mother had given him of our current Milway project. I'd been reticent with him about the digging, too restrained not wanting to trouble him or make him feel he was missing out on something important.

"Entrance, "I answered. We're taking the grassy top off the

main cave area today. All of this dried out weedy area," I pointed to the spot as I spoke.

Ricky arrived soon after that, alone again, and started right in to digging inside the large circle area that we'd marked-off throughout the dried, and wilted brown weeds.

"Throw it far past the edge," I reminded him. "We'll need a clear foot all the way around to set the planks that are gonna hold the roof."

We dug as Billy watched. We worked at it until I had to stop digging and attend to my paper route. Some days I was almost too tired to pedal my bike, and my paper route seemed to have grown longer. The houses all seemed to be much further away from each other after I'd spent hours digging.

*   *   *

During the night, being mesmerized by the blinking intersection light that I could see from out of my bedroom window, I'd decided to dig a Y-section near the end of the entrance. One tunnel would go to the main cave; the other would be a dead end trap for unwelcome visitors. As I lay in my sweat watching the blinking light, listening to the cicadas trying to announce a premature end to summer, I felt only one breath of fresh air slide over my bare legs and chest. I knew it wasn't any barometric change or trickle of a west wind. No, I was fully aware that it was old Time sneaking in to encourage me to work faster on this most marvelous endeavor of the summer. It was to be the biggest project ever, bigger even than any previous or future winter snow fort or igloo, bigger than any hut we'd ever built, or would build. This was our Hanging Garden of Babylon, our Pyramid, and our First Wonder of the World. I sensed that Time wanted us to succeed, but He had to remind us that being twelve cannot last forever…even though it should.

During the following morning, Billy joined us, but could only sit and watch us as Ricky removed the entire grassy top section of where we would dig much deeper to make our cave. I began digging out the new forked tunnel part of the ditch off the real burrow entrance to our cave. I could tell Billy was bothered by not being able to help, but his presence there helped bond our effort, and increased our determination to complete this project.

Anthony arrived just in time to help me finish the Y section of the entrance, and then he squared off the sides of our ditch, which was now nearly three feet deep. I suggested we leave the first two feet a little higher than the rest of the entrance to help keep out any rainwater that might possibly flood in.

"Good idea," Billy said in support.

"Okay, we can cover that part too," Anthony said. He, like me, wanted to see things get done quickly, sometimes too fast. He helped me lay some of the staves across the very start of the ditch at our cave's entrance. We put the curved sides upward giving us even more headroom to crawl through. Tarpaper went on next, and then we both shoveled the dirt from along the sides of the ditch back over the roofing. We had about two feet of entrance done before lunchtime. Beneath was a cooling shaded area. It helped foreshadow the satisfaction of a fully completed cave. For the first time since I had had the conception of a cave in Milway, I felt encouraged enough to anticipate success. We might soon be able to revert into being Neanderthals, and no one would even know that we did. We'd beat the seasonal sun at its own game like Cro-Magnons did to the wintery ice; caves were the solution to living better in summer, and in the winter as well. Besides being Prince of the pepper field, I'd be the King of the cave. I don't know when those types of thoughts faded, but they did, and I don't expect them to ever return. I would soon have an epiphany that would steal a lot of my youthful thinking.

Only Ricky and I were working later that afternoon. We stopped digging, sat together in the tiny covered section of the entrance talking about everything else we'd need, and then we began to roam around Milway seeking lumber that we'd use to cover the main cavern area. There was an old cedar pole my uncle Mike used years ago when pulling up an old well to replace the point. The point is the five-foot piece of pipe where the screen is that let's well-water come into the pipe. Then, a hand or power pump can suck up the water from its underground stream. One of the largest natural underground aquifers anywhere is under the New Jersey Pinelands Region, and Milway is located right at the southern edge of that enormous aquifer.

I had used a hand-pump many times and loved to prime it, work the water up in the vacuum of the pipe, and then, holding one hand over the pump's mouth, fill it with refreshing water right from its underground stream. It always tasted better than water that had been stored in a tank waiting to be used. Drinking water from a hand-pump was almost as good as slurping an ice cream soda. It smelled like wet clover right after a spring shower. It had a mineral aroma. Fresh well water was really a divine nectar, a drink for the gods. My father always called water, "Adam's Ale." I had no idea that in the future, I'd buy bottled water, in plastic, not glass, that would cost more than a gallon of gasoline.

After we carried the old cedar pole back to the cave site, we returned to the barn and pumped ourselves a refreshing drink instead of just using the back yard garden hose with water taken from the tank in the basement of my house. My uncles had started tearing down the animal sheds from along side the barn, but they left the pump, and the half-barrel below it that had always stored water for the animals to drink. They left the pump thinking they just might have to use it again. They never did. Only I used it. I used it nearly everyday until my uncles took off the hand-pump, and pulled up the pipe to save the point at the bottom. That was another thing they never used again.

Ricky left for the day, and then I went to deliver my newspapers. When I rode by Billy's house, I saw him taking careful steps in his side yard. I guessed that he'd be over first thing tomorrow, and maybe be able to help with some of the cave's construction. I was right.

Everybody, all the guys that is, had now heard about our cave even though the main area was only about six inches deep. The front tunnel, however, was down a full three feet, and the false tunnel that turned off at the Y-intersection dipped another six inches making it look like the correct entrance into the main cavity. Our youngest helpers, Philip and Jo-Jo, along with Gary, helped drag back some of the dirt from the cave's edge. For every shovel full we pitched out, they'd drag away at least half of it. We needed to set lumber over the massive hole to make a roof, or we wouldn't end up with an enclosed cave. We dug. We scraped into the earth. I even brought a pick to the site so when we hit stony and hard gravely spots, we could loosen the soil enough to scoop it up, and heave it onto the grass around our marked-out circle. We dug most of the morning. There wasn't a single cloud in the blue-baked sky to shade us. Ricky worked the hardest. I dug and kept the engineering design squared-off along all the edges. The sidewalls of our cave would be perfectly perpendicular to the ground around it. Anthony dug too. He worked harder that day than ever before. Sensing a conclusion always helped to motivate his enthusiasm. My cousin Billy stopped by with Jackie just to check out what they'd heard from the girls who'd been watching us from a distance across the railroad tracks. Nimble-footed Billy got there just before our lunch break, stepped away from his bike, and limped toward us. Then, he hobbled around laying out some of the wood we'd collected for the roof. The nail holes in his feet were quickly healing.

"Hey. Look. A sea shell," proclaimed Ricky, as he flipped a shovel full of dirt up onto the grass.

We all stopped working and went to examine it. As I cleaned the orange-colored gravel off of it, I saw my mother heading across the street to my grandmother's. Grandmom Anna had been ill for a while now, but sickness was something that came and went quickly in our young world. My mother had spent the past two days visiting her more often than usual. Twice I noticed a number of different automobiles at my grandmother's house, but I mostly ignored them. The last thing I wanted to do was having to wash-up and visit neighbors and relatives I didn't really know very well. I was constructing a cave. I had no time for anything else.

"What do you call those guys who dig up old stuff in Egypt?" asked Ricky.

"Archeologists," I answered. I must have heard some grownup use the word.

Our entire team of workers turned and stared at me because of my answer. I had no idea where I heard or read about them, but I knew it was correct. No one asked another question about it.

"Start looking at everything you toss up. Maybe we found an ancient city," Ricky said.

"My uncle Foxy told me that all this land was under the ocean once," I said. "Maybe this was the beach?"

"Maybe," repeated Billy. "Or, maybe somebody just had a clam bake out here."

The channeled Duck Clam shell could have been from some clambake, but then it would have been buried just a few inches below the surface, not two feet down. We looked much more carefully as we dug during the next half hour checking and searching for other Molluscan seashells. I found a stone structure that, at first, looked like a Gastropod, but it wasn't. It was only a rock. I later brought up a cocoon of some sorts that I first thought might have been a Nautilus shell, but once again, it turned out to be only the remains of some land-dwelling creature. I had read about early cavemen using some seashells as tools, but nothing we found was ever used by any caveman, nor did we find any other shells. I think we were all a little disappointed to not have found any more seashells. If we did, I thought, our cave site would have been even more special.

"Probably came from just a clambake," Billy announced once again.

"Most likely," said Ricky.

Only I stuck hard fast to the idea that this field we were standing on was once the bottom of an ocean. Maybe we were on the beach of that ancient ocean. That theory wasn't confirmed until many years later, and by then, I could get no satisfaction from having been correct.

Again, Billy said, " Just some shell from a clambake. Popeye probably dumped them here." Everybody, even the youngsters in town called my uncle Joe, Popeye.

That conclusion took away the magic of the find. We tossed the shell away, possibly exposing it to direct sunshine in over a million, maybe ten million years, and then returned to our digging. Our entrance tunnels were ready to be covered completely. Again, it made us feel like a lot of progress was being made. We ran out of barrel staves, and had to put parts of old nail-filled two-by-sixes across the fresh new ditch, and then lay irregular pieces of plywood on them covering the tunnel. We lost the arched dome that we had near the opening created by the curved barrel staves, but we had dug the concluding part of the entrance tunnel section deeper, so it didn't really affect the amount of headroom.

Anthony had to leave about that time, and so did everyone else, except Ricky and me. Together, we covered the newly set roof with all the dirt along side the trench, and smoothed it off with the rake that I brought to the site for the first time that morning. Ricky stuck a few clusters of grass that we'd dug out back into the dirt over the tunnel. If it grows, I thought, it would camouflage everything, and make it look like a natural cave, one that's been here since the seashells were being washed up on a beach or washed back into the sea.

Except for its Y-shape, our entrance tunnel now looked like a mounded gravesite.

I first noticed Billy's new sneaks when he had to leave and head home for lunch, and then again as he peddled his bike back home. The swelling in his feet had shrunk a lot, and now, walking seemed to help him. He'd be digging as soon as he could put his foot on a shovel. When we heard the drilling-pitch of the noon time siren singing out by the fire hall, Ricky and I put our shovels down into the circular pit, now nearly three feet deep all the way across the area we'd marked off, and then each of us silently headed home to eat. Cave construction creates enormous appetites, and miniscule conversations.

When I got back to my house, I saw my mother's eyes had been watering as she made me two, not one, peanut butter and grape jelly sandwiches. I told her I was starving when I got into the kitchen. She asked what we're doing, and I told her we were playing Archeologist. She stared at me for a few seconds, just like the guys outside had done, and then went about her own business.

We never lied when we were twelve, but we never told the whole truth. Any specifics were always best left unstated. The more you said, the more you had to explain.

We said very little to make our parents worry. We knew too much concern would add too many restrictions. None of us needed to be told to not play in, on, or around Billy's father's old demolished chicken coop. Experience taught us that. No one ever thought again to take a bow and arrow near his house. People who don't learn from their mistakes don't survive. That's why kids have to be free to make mistakes. To fall, to get cut, to scrape their knees, even to get stung by bees. They're all educational moments. We learned, I think, far more during our summer vacations than what we ever learned during the school year. Gaining knowledge during the summer diminishes as we grow, and school, I'm sorry to say, seems to teach lots of facts, but very little thinking. That's the most important skill of all: thinking. In every field of study: math, history, English, in every subject, it's thinking skills, basic logic, which should be the real goal. It doesn't happen much anymore, I'm afraid.

That afternoon, only Ricky and I dug for a while, but we tired quickly. The burnt sea-blue sky was not only cloudless, it was birdless too. Nothing moved in town. We quit digging, and sat in the cooler shade of the section of the tunnel we had already finished, the entrance that was covered over, and talked about how neat it would be when it was all finished. It was late in the afternoon by then, and Ricky had to return home because he had eggs to pick, and I wanted to wash the gray clay and orange gravel off my arms before I biked away to deliver my newspapers.

That night, there was a lot of activity downstairs as I tried to fall asleep. I heard people come and go. I could hear cars pull into the driveway across the street. The last thing I heard was the late train flying by our cave site north toward Philadelphia. There was nothing on the rails to be flattened, so it easily sped along. In the morning I learned that my Grandmother had died.

13-A

"Roll out the barrel, we'll have a barrel of fun," sang Frankie Yankovic, bellowing out from our radio every Saturday morning in my mother's kitchen. I got a kick out of his, *In Heaven There Is No Beer*, singing: "and when we're gone from here, all our friends will be drinking all our beer." The Bridgeton radio station hosted three full hours of polka music every Saturday morning; my mother never missed it, not even once. From a nation where the people had been conquered and suppressed so often, came a music that was so filled with the joys of life. A weekend morning that starts with polka music will be a weekend filled with fun and happiness. I still play a little polka music on Saturdays and even on some Sunday mornings, especially if I have a guest visiting. In the evenings of my more mature years, I'll have a sparkling wine instead of a beer, but so what!

Since my mother always had to work on Saturday mornings, she played the Polkas loud enough for her to hear two rooms over in the Post Office section of our house. It was actually loud enough to hear more than two rooms away. *Helena Polka, Pennsylvania Polka*, and my favorite one, the *Clarinet Polka*. Nothing picks up a sleeping drowsy morning like Polka music. You seem to absorb the music into your blood-flow and into your brain. If the music were playing, my mother would skip any English words, and say, *Dzien Dobry*, in

Polish, instead of good morning to me. I almost always had Snap, Crackle, and Pop in my cereal bowl, and I listened to them many times during the week, but on Saturdays, the Polka music drowned them out. They were mute inside my breakfast bowl, and they remained silent until I finished my breakfast.

I understood all the sights and sounds of life, but nothing about the solitude of death. That magician friend of Time lowers a dark veil and the person is gone. Very few people ever teach about all the magic involved with life. No one ever gives any instructions on the magic of death.

When I was really quite young, four or five, I think, I was playing in my Grandmother's back yard. All I can recall is that she, like my mother, let me run free. The chicken that was chasing me, the one that kept bothering and tormenting me, turned and pecked at my face. It stuck its beak right into my right eyebrow. My Grandmother quickly washed it clean of blood, and then put a Band-Aid along side of my right eye. Right after she helped bandage me up, she returned to the back yard, and caught the chicken by its legs. She hung it upside down as she walked over to a stump right by the back door, and with a hatchet, cut off its head. She dropped the bird to the ground and I watched the headless chicken run around her backyard sprinting in circles without running into anything. It missed the clothesline poles, and even the side of the small chicken coop. It nearly missed one of the poles supporting the fence that kept the chickens from running off. Headless, and spurting blood, it ran and ran until it dropped. She then began to pluck the feathers, and immediately started to prepare it for my grandfather's dinner. To this day, I never knew if that bird was being punished for trying to blind me, or if it would have routinely become my grandfather's dinner.

My Grandmother Anna came from Krakow, Poland as a young girl, and never went home again. I remember her round Polish face always had a smile on it. She had long silky straight hair hanging down past her shoulders. It was all as white as snow when I was twelve. Only now that I realize Milway will always be with me, can I understand how she must have kept a little of Krakow in her heart. She liked my mother's Saturday morning Polka music as much as I did, and she seemed to be thinking about some place else, somewhere far away, whenever she heard it. I believe that when the Polka music was playing, she could visit her home in her mind, and maybe thought about when she was twelve years old. None of her ten children ever got to play in Krakow. They all grew up in Milway. After what the Nazis did to Poland, I'm sure she was quite happy about that.

Much later I learned that most birds try to blind their victims when first attacking them. They go for the eyes. It's easier to conquer a sightless enemy. Ulysses proved that with the Cyclops. I was at fault for irritating the chicken, and I wondered why that simpleton brother of Time, silly Luck, saved me again from a lifetime of being blind in one eye.

I played no role in the funeral activities during the next four days, and the more I kept busy on my own, the easier it was for my mother. Billy was walking easily again, without any pain, so he, Ricky, and I spent the remainder of the week digging out the cave. For the first time that I could ever remember, there was no Polka music playing in the house on the Saturday of my Grandmother's funeral. The weekend came and went without any music at all. Years later, when I buried my own mother, I played the *Helena Polka* during her funeral mass, right after the sermon. It helped everyone in the church feel a little better; especially me.

Grief is like a heavy dark blanket blacking out everything in sight. Later on in life I learned that the blacker the night, the brighter are the stars, and grief helps you remember all the bright shiny things about the person you lost. With all the bad things we hear about the passing of time, one good thing Time does is help grief diminish without removing any of the positive memories. "Roll out the barrel, we'll have a barrel of fun…"

14

Nearly all the younger kids, and even Anthony stopped visiting the enormous hole, the crater-like depression, which we'd been digging for days and days that to some of us felt like months and months. Ricky, Billy, and I had the central cavern down nearly four feet deep. That was more than enough to crawl around in. The deeper we dug, the easier it got to push a shovel into the virgin earth. The only hard part for us was to lift and toss the dirt up over the edge of the cave's wall, and far enough away so it didn't slide back down. With the younger guys all gone, we had no one around to scrape the top edge away as we had when we first started.

We found that digging in the morning was the best time to work. The blistering August afternoons weakened us too quickly. None of us ever remember summer's heat or winter's cold; we just remembered doing things: playing games, building forts, climbing up the new mountain of coal when my uncle refilled the bins, playing basketball against the barn, and riding our bikes to the gravel pits, fire-crackers, kites, and playing baseball, or Kick-the-Can. Now, after doing the same thing day after day, we grew weary. Would everybody give up before it's finished I wondered? I just won't let it happen was what I dreamed almost every night as I lay sweating on my bed yearning for a breath of fresh air to blow in from any of the opened windows. My smaller bedroom window faced south, and the other larger window faced west. There was no sign of any natural relief. No one had air-conditioning back then. We needed a cave, not just to play in, or to hide from the summer's blistering heat, no, after so many days of working on this site, I simply thought that Milway just ought to have a cave. No place else in South Jersey did.

It must have been the same people who were making the trip from Philadelphia to the Jersey shore; Ocean City or maybe Cape May, nearly everyday. We always stopped digging when a train went by. Like always, we counted the number of boxcars that were on any freight train flowing by hoping for a new record. The silver passenger trains usually had just three cars, and we let them speed by without doing any counting. During the August heat spell, the passenger trains many times had four cars, still not worth counting. We noticed more people waving to us each day. They seemed to have become a part of the construction inspectors who were watching us digging day after day. What's it going to be, I'm sure they wondered. We had more than a dump truck of dirt piled up all around the cave site. It must have looked like a new house was being built in plain sight just across the field from the railroad tracks.

Ricky wanted to put on the roof and be done with it. Billy took his side. I said that we should do it right. Once the roof is over the cave, and covered with the dirt, we wouldn't be able to dig anymore without crawling in and out with buckets. "Too hard," I told them both. "Once we have the roof on, and the entire cave area covered with dirt, and we decide that we need it to be deeper, who wants to crawl out with buckets of dirt over and over again?" I asked them both.

Neither responded in the affirmative, but neither of my pals were happy about doing any more digging during the hottest days of the year.

Then just when my laborers were ready to rebel, I got a labor saving idea. "Hey, we're almost deep enough. Let's leave a foot-high bench of gravel all the way around inside the cave." I dragged my shovel to make a mark. "We'll just take it down from this smaller circle, and then we'll have a place to sit, a place to store stuff. We'll have a natural shelf to put things on."

"Hey, that'll be a lot less dirt to dig out," said Billy changing his support, as he watched me draw a much smaller circle on the cave floor with the handle of my shovel.

"Okay," Ricky said. "Let's see what it will look like." He started digging a shovel-wide trench around the circle I had marked off. Billy and I dug up the center so within another half hour, we had the foot-wide dirt bench all the way around our cave's main chamber, and had dug the floor about four or five inches below the bench level.

I knew we had to go deeper, but I really wanted either of them to make the next suggestion, so I said that we could quit digging right there.

"That's not high enough to sit on," Ricky said. "The floor has to be lower or our knees will be hitting our chins."

"Yea," agreed Billy. "Just one more shovel deeper, and we've got it."

Only the tops of our heads were now scarcely showing above the enormous crater's upper most edge. People in the trains going by could never see us if we didn't climb out for each passing caravan, and be able to wave back to the all the curious people. The entranceway to our cave had already been covered, so they couldn't see any open trench anymore.

Ricky and Billy were happy about us being almost done. I was happy I got them to agree with me, and was even more pleased to have had them try to convince me to keep digging. At last I understood the philosophy behind Tom Sawyer getting his friends to help him paint Aunt Polly's fence. I told them that tomorrow we could start covering the entire cave. For a number of days now we had quit laboring well before sunset because of the heat spell we'd been having. I hoped it would stay hot forever because very soon, only we would have a cool place to hide from the vindictive sun.

All three of us worked way past the noontime fire whistle, and had to make our own sandwiches when we each returned home. Instead of playing stickball after dinner, we decided to return to the cave site in the cool of the evening, and maybe dig a little more.

*   *   *

We didn't dig. Not even a single shovel full. We entered from the drainage bank. We crawled through the already finished entrance tunnel, going past the fake Y, and right down into the central cavity. On our tiptoes, we could see the edge of dead grass all the way around our dugout circle. The surrounding dirt piles prevented us from seeing any further. An enemy ambush of invading Apaches could be gathering to attack, but we'd never see them. Martians might have landed in the same field as our cave, but we'd have never seen them. After we all sat down on the dirt, they both asked me about my Grandmother, but I didn't have much to say. There wasn't anything about death that I knew about or could fully understand. I told them she was in the ground buried next to her youngest son Eddie. Gangsters, or strikebreakers in New York murdered him during the Great Depression long before I was even born. I never got the entire truth. My mother, and each uncle, all had a slightly different version about what happened to Uncle Eddie. I also doubted there was ever a time before I was born. It's too hard to figure out, and tiring to think about any time before your own, so I changed the subject and suggested that when we get it all covered, we try to replant lots of grass and weeds over the top.

"Yes! Disguise it, " Billy said. "We'll be the only people who'll know it's here." He added that he had some grass seed at home. We used it the same day we finished covering the cave, and we were fortunate to have it rain on the seeds that same night. We would see it growing within a week.

That was a motion presented, discussed, and voted on. It carried unanimously. We'd try to disguise the greatest construction project Milway had ever had. There was no reason for having grownups try to scare us about all the dangerous possibilities: bad air to breathe, cave-ins, or wild animals attacking us inside. No, we'd made it ourselves, and we'd keep it to ourselves. It was a pact of the brotherhood. The first and only Milway cave just had to be hidden. Once the new grass grew over the top of our cave, the grownups would quickly forget about it. The motion would be enacted.

That evening we experienced the coolest dusk in over two weeks. Maybe the weather would change. If it rained before we got it completely covered, I feared we'd have a real muddy mess, but the little weather clip presented each day on the upper front page of the papers I delivered, said nothing about rain. It fact, it reported that the reprieve from the sun's torture was just a brief retreat from a future of burning hot days. We'd have a cool underground retreat into which we could escape Apollo's revenge. To be on the safe side, the people predicting the weather always say there is a chance, no matter how slight, of a passing thunderstorm. That actually did happen the night after we concluded our work and had spread Billy's grass seed over the finished cave roof, but the rainfall was over in a matter of minutes. Nothing would run through the soft dirt on the roof of the cave; it was just enough water to kick-start the grass seeds into growing.

Stickball and Kick-the-Can competitions were reduced from

an hour or more to just thirty-minute contests every evening during the heat wave. The blistering weather seemed necessary to slow people down, and give them all time to grieve, and adjust to Milway without my Grandmother Anna. I hadn't seen my Grandfather, George, since long before we started working on the cave, and the last time I was with him anywhere was in his blacksmith's shop in the barn. That had been much earlier in the summer, at least a month or more ago. I had no idea how he was doing, or how he felt about the passing of his wife. At twelve years old, who would want to concern themselves with grownup feelings?

The following day, Ricky had to go with his family to Vineland. Billy had to visit relatives in Ways Cove for one of his cousin's birthday. I didn't want to dig alone. I helped mow some of the back yard. I picked the first cantaloupe of the season. It was not ripe enough to enjoy. I pulled some of the weeds around my mother's flowers that grew in our back yard. Mostly I just lingered around the house waiting for lunch. So, after the usual peanut butter and jelly sandwich, for a rare luncheon dessert, my mother opened a Mason jar of this year's peaches. "Eat slowly," she told me. "And, only one bowl. We'll have the rest after supper." This broke the tradition of opening the first jar of peaches during the first cold spell when we saw not green, but frosted white grass in the morning. Something told me that her life had completely changed; she was so different, but I said nothing about it because I didn't understand it. Years later, I'd experience a similar metamorphosis.

For some reason, she seemed to think that I was holding back some remorse, some sadness, like what she was feeling, so she wanted to brighten my attitude by offering me a treat that I'd usually have to wait for until after the first frost to enjoy. Each slice on my spoon made me recall the days we picked, skinned, and canned the preserved peaches. Time stands still in a quart jar of peaches. The sugar seemed sweeter than when I first bit into them. They were a darker gold already, and as I ate each peach slice, I could hear whispers coming back from the conversations we had on the day we canned them. How could that be? I knew there was a wonder deep in the nearby woods, fascinating things in the barn, the hayloft, and in the shop. I knew the potato house was mysterious, and odd things happened in the chicken coops where we hunted rats, but where did the voices come from in my mother's kitchen? I pondered. I looked and checked to see if the radio was off. It was off. The only explanation for the conversations I was hearing was that Old Man Time was free from any serious obligations, and was just teasing me. Maybe he was checking to see if I was still twelve. Maybe it was just the sweet peach flavor rising and changing from aroma to sound just like when Billy and I heard the sounds of all the colors around us when we lay in my front yard near dusk as we waited for the appearance of the first star. We heard the flame-green grass, the blue-black sky, and the yellow and gray shades of painted houses. We saw, tasted, touched, smelled, and heard everything around us as only boys of twelve can do. I don't know when I lost the ability to do that, but I did.

*　　　*　　　*

Funeral feelings disappear in children as quickly as they spring upon us. I was aware, however, that my aunts and uncles, along with my mother, were much quieter than usual, and that they really wanted to be left alone for a while. I helped simply by getting out of the house, and went back to our cave site as often as possible.

We started the final construction by digging out the remainder of the floor. Ricky raked it smooth, and he even pulled the rake through the entrance tunnel sections that were already completed. Billy and I set the long cedar pole across the center of the cavern.

"More to your right," I cried to Billy. "Keep it parallel to the railroad tracks so the vibrations the trains make won't shake and loosen the boards sitting on top of it."

"Okay," he said.

"Good thinking," Ricky told me.

We all began to place pieces of old plywood, parts of the sidewall of the chicken coop where Billy nailed himself down, and the two large metal signs over the slats running from the cedar pole to the outer most edge of the cave. We covered the sections nearest the entrance tunnels first. Then we put as much tarpaper over the wood that we could find. We used the old shingles I'd wheel-barrowed to the cave more than a week earlier to cover all around the center, overlapping the cedar pole and the plywood covering it. No water would ever leak through that part of the roof. After we had about three quarters of the cave's roof covered, we all started to shovel the dirt encircling the big hole back onto its original location. We covered all the wood nearest to the entrance first. We'd rest. Walk to the entrance, and see it getting darker and darker inside. Then shovel some more. The vast opening in the earth was disappearing.

Before the lunchtime siren went off, we had everything, except one small area that was still uncovered with wood, covered over with dirt. Except for that small section, the size of a floor mat, we had all the rest of it covered with a thick load of Milway dirt. The vast piles of noticeable soil were now just a small slanted mound of sand and gravel, which was slightly showing through the high weeds that were growing over the rest of the field.

After lunch, it took the three of us nearly three hours to find just the right piece of wood to cover the remaining tiny opening in our cave's roof.

"Think this will fit?" asked Billy pointing to some old one-by-fours.

"No," said Ricky.

"How about that window frame? He suggested once more.

"No," said Ricky again. "It has to be one piece.

"Yes," I said. "One piece if possible. It's only as wide as a small door, and about half as long."

"A door," said Ricky with the tone of answering a question to a teacher. "We saw a half door back inside the old factory. Downstairs along side the glass blocks."

We both remembered it. It was strange to see a full door that had been cut in half. They must have used it for a small tabletop, or only had a small area to work in, and simply cut an old unused door in half giving it a useful life once again.

"Let's go get it," I said. "Ricky and I can do it," I said to Billy. "You stay here and finish covering the rest of this section. Save enough dirt to cover the half-door when we get back."

We'd resurrected the old door once again. It may have been reborn as a tabletop, but now it was gong to be a section of roof for the best cave ever. You have to look at things, try to see what they can become, and not always simply judge them for what they are. Teachers are supposed to do that, but they many times don't.

We headed off across the tracks walking quickly to the old factory. The afternoon was flying by, and I'd have to leave soon to work my paper route. I rushed Ricky as much as possible because I could sense the conclusion of our project.

The half door was exactly where we'd seen it earlier in the summer. Together we carried it out the side door, down to and across the railroad tracks, and up the embankment toward the cave. It was the final piece. We held it up like an Olympic torch. Billy cheered. We quickly set it in place and Billy started to throw dirt on it before we could even put some tarpaper over it.

"Hold it," I said. "Tarpaper." Without it, the door would quickly rot, and have its multi-purpose life come too quickly to an end.

After using the last of the tarpaper, Billy excitedly covered it all by himself. Ricky raked the remaining gravel into a level area on top, and then raked some clusters of dirt downward to mesh with the grass that had been covered with our digging spoils for some days now.

The damp dirt, taken from well below the surface, would all dry out quickly as the surrounding grass would revive, and new weeds would grow over the entire roof of the first and only cave Milway ever had. We tossed Billy's grass seeds over all the bare spots.

We all went to the entrance and crawled in. The three of us blocked any light from the entrance so we couldn't see anything until we all got into the main chamber, and then turned our bodies toward the entrance. The Y curve of the tunnel blocked a lot of outside light, but the chamber quickly filled with a warm glow of success. It was already cooler down there than outside in the sun. Everybody would be there tomorrow morning. I'd bring a candle, I told them both.

"I'll see if I can get a flashlight," Ricky said.

The rain shower we had that night was hardly heavy enough to wash the dust off the tree leaves, but it would kick-start the growth of our grass seeds. The cave site would be completely invisible to passengers on the trains, and to anyone driving by. As the weeds grew higher, they would hide the mounded hill we had to create as we covered the roof of the cave.

Everyone showed up the following morning. There were six of us inside the main chamber. Ricky, Anthony, and I sat on the ledge of gravel that we hadn't dug out. The ledge circled around the entire wall of the cave. All the others sat on the orange gravel cave floor.

"We need a rug," said Tudor, using the word *we* like he was a major part of our new family of cave dwellers.

I quickly saw the possibility of covering the cave floor. It would prevent a lot of gravelly stains on our knees and backsides and keep our mothers happier. By winter, I thought, we may even need to protect ourselves from the cold, so a rug might really help.

"We've got some old chicken feed bags. You know, the brown burlap bags," Ricky added.

"There's a piece of rug in our farm shed," Billy said. "I'll get it this afternoon. I don't know how big it is, but it'll cover a good part of this dirt floor."

"We'll put the feed bags under it, and maybe on the ledge so we can sit on them," I interjected.

"Good idea," said Ricky.

"And more candles," Anthony added. "We can't burn a lantern in here. We might gas ourselves."

No one had thought of that. We knew you weren't supposed to burn your kerosene heaters inside the house for too long without letting in fresh air. None of us knew much about carbon monoxide, but we'd all heard the adults around us discussing the danger of heaters.

Each of us carried shovels, picks, and rakes back to where we'd gotten them when we first started working on our Neanderthal site. There was nothing left to do after lunch except try to make the inside more comfortable. Tudor borrowed a battery flashlight from his father's gas station. I think it is still buried in the heart of the cave. I know we never returned it that summer.

*   *   *

Not as many people came to visit the hidden cave as had come to visit the igloo we'd built during the biggest winter snowstorm Milway had ever seen; well the biggest I had ever seen. Few of us ever talked about the long cold spell that would follow the waning summer. Now always wins out over the past or the future. Passengers on the trains heading down to the shore, or back to the city, quickly tired of standing at the passenger car windows for a glimpse of our project. From the train, it had all disappeared. A thunderstorm that night helped break the heat spell. More importantly, it inspired a quick new spurt in the grass growth, and wild weed progression. In just one short week, vegetation was making the cave site invisible to everyone who didn't see the tunnel entrance or know about what we'd dug.

After we covered the floor with chicken feed bags, and topped it off with the old piece of carpet Billy delivered, the cave was completed. It quickly became a retreat from not only the heat, but from whatever games we were playing. It seemed we'd always find time for a cave-break from our games, especially on the hotter days of the fading summer.

None of us knew that my mother had walked out to inspect what we'd dug while I was biking my paper route. She began asking some of the local men if they thought it was safe. None of them were about to crawl inside to inspect it, but they all told her if it caved in, it could smoother us. That was hardly the truth, but it began to weigh heavily on my mother. As I look back, I can understand why my mother had magnified her concerns over my welfare. It was just too soon since Grandmom Anna was taken away from us.

Billy was walking perfectly again with no after effects of being nailed to the chicken coop wood. I could tell that he could ride his bike easily again, so I suggested we bike to my uncle Foxy's place on the way to Dorothy, the first town south of Milway. He said that he had to help his father with something in their yard, so we had to wait until the next day. After a few days of cave dwelling, Tudor and Anthony, along with Philip and Jo-Jo tired of meeting inside the cave to discuss any future plans. The heat spell had passed and cave retreats became less necessary to avoid the burning sun. Ricky and I wanted to dig another fake entrance tunnel, but Billy was tired of digging so we never started it. I noticed changes in our gang's attitude whenever we completed some task like raking the basketball court clean of stones, or making a wooden tepee. Looking back, I first noticed how quickly apathy grew when we tried to make a maze in the rye field across from Spitz's gas station running along side the chicken coop where Billy had his fateful encounter, during his conflict with Luck's cousin Chance, and that rusty pair of nails.

Apathy always won out over continued enthusiasm.

Summer was fading quickly now, but Time prevented any of us from noticing it. His crazy brother Luck, who sometimes helped you, and other times hurt you, hadn't been around in quite a while, so I was happy that no one was there to interfere with our freedom.

Milway had a cave. That was all Billy and I thought about.

15

Making a maze without power mowers, or an overhead view of the entire field was another major engineering feat attempted by my friends and me. The real fun is in making it, and not running through it afterwards. I understood why; the closer we got to finishing it, the faster our gang became apathetic about it. I've come to believe that is true whether you're twelve, forty, or eighty. Life itself can be anti-climatic so spend as much time with Chance's younger sister as you can. Remember, Joy also sneaks away very quickly; usually at the first opportunity she gets. The older I got, the less I could do what I wanted to do. I was told once that a person's final words are too many times their saddest statements. No one on their deathbed has ever uttered as their final words, "Gee, I wish I could have worked more." The challenge of doing anything is always more important than the conclusion.

The cave had taken a lot of work. It tired us out, and excited us at the same time. Now, whenever we were doing anything that might quickly bore us, we could retreat back to the cave and relax inside the cool earth while we made plans for another adventure. Maze making wouldn't take anywhere near as long as building a fort or digging a cave. We simply had to keep track of where the road was, how far away we wanted the exit to be, and then stomp through the tall rye grass turning left and right so it wouldn't be an easy escape for first-timers. The tall grass was always six inches to a full foot higher than our heads. First of all, we'd zigzag a trail from the start to the end. Then, we'd march through and make some short dead-end walkways after making at least one right turn, and then one or two left turns. The perfect dead-end had at least two turns in it before the hiker found no place left to go.

We'd make mazes right after school during the first warm spring evenings, and then again late in the summer, when the rye was once again tall enough so that we could not see over it. I'd have Ricky walk along the roadside and shout to me repeatedly so I'd know how far I was from the edge of the rye field. Billy, who was the same height as me, but heavier, would bulldoze down the stalks that I missed as I walked through ahead of him. Together, we'd make a walkway straight in, then walk left for ten or fifteen steps before going right. After that, we'd go forward, then another right heading backward, before making a left, and then another left. I'd try to not repeat any pattern as Billy and I marked out a roadway from the entrance to the exit turning the field of rye into a green maze. As soon as the two of us walked back out onto the road at the maze's exit, Ricky would join us making offshoot pathways along each length of a straight route having at least one turn in it before stopping at a dead-end. All of our mazes were different every time we made one, but with careful inspection anyone could see the more worn pathway that lead to the exit. It was just like Robert Frost's poem, "The Road Not Taken," where one roadway was worn less, and wanted, even begged for travelers, but the other roadway, which was worn down the most, was the choice of the majority of so many lost, weary travelers. If Mr. Frost had been in our maze, he would never have gotten out because he'd take the path less traveled.

The goal of the game was to enter and exit the fastest. We'd all count out loud as someone started. We'd have people at the start and the finish. The most fun was when younger kids came to run their way through it. We'd never do it faster even though we knew it better; we'd always let one of the younger kids win. I was the fastest runner in our group, and could easily remember the route Billy and I first made. I could quite easily win every time we played there, but I had learned that summer that winning isn't always the most important thing. Sharing the excitement of success is many times a much better feeling than winning.

The maze certainly wasn't the most exciting thing during the summer of the bees, the rope across Billy's neck, the arrow in his arm, and the nails he'd jumped on. The hayloft, and the cave were much more important items on my agenda. The times that stuck with Billy the most, and also with me, were the quiet evenings when we spread out on the grass on my front lawn, and looked up toward the heavens. Questioning is something every kid does naturally; grownups stifle that skill because it annoys them.

We would run the maze, and then call for Kick-the-Can. After that, Billy and I would meander to my front yard, and check out the Big Dipper while lying on our sweaty backs. We'd wait without the slightest movement until either one of our mothers called for us. Summer just stood still for both of us; we knew that we had forever to count the stars, and every single silent evening, we would try to spot a new one. We spotted more and more shooting starts as the month of August began to fade into history, but we never noticed any new star that we hadn't seen before. Our adult eyes can't tell the difference among any stars anymore.

*　　　*　　　*

During the following week, the blistering hot days cooled to a full week of pleasant balmy summer sunlit hours. We had no need to retreat into our cave so Ricky and I ventured into the sweet potato house. We moved some empty wooden crates to the side, and then lifted others above us as we worked our way into the large stack of wooden boxes. About five crates in, we pulled a few out and placed them above the walkway we'd made. Very easily, and quite fast compared to digging the cave, we had a mini hidden fort. The place would be perfect for future hide and seek games, or to use as a base for future commando raids.

I usually worried about my grandfather chasing me out of his potato storage building, but I hadn't seen my grandfather since long before my grandmother passed away, and Ricky and I both felt safe playing where we shouldn't be playing at all. He had disappeared from the shop in the barn, from all of the nearby fields, and he hadn't even come to chase us away from digging our cave along side one of his major gardens. I never asked why he wasn't showing himself. My mother, and all my uncles, had been rather subdued since the passing of my grandmother. There was less talking in Milway, and more hand, eye, and head gesturing it seemed to me. Even the morning symposiums of Milway's philosophic businessmen was shortened and much quieter.

*   *   *

The sweet potato harvest would begin in less than two months, and our restructuring of the stacks of potato crates would certainly make it more difficult for my uncles to move them outside, and then carry them down to the potato fields on Millville Avenue, or to the other large sweet potato field down toward East Boundary Avenue on the way to Ways Cove. I report this in retrospection; at the time there was no concern with causing anyone any trouble. Whatever was on our minds at the moment was the most important thing in the world, and we never worried about causing any problems for any grownups. It was they who almost always caused problems for us.

I had learned to steer a truck during the previous sweet potato harvest. The men would pick the potatoes and fill the wooden crates. They would leave them all along the rows. After all the picking and crate-packing was done, they would drive very slowly down every fourth row with the old Ford flat-body truck, and load all the filled potato crates onto the truck. Late in the season during that most eventful year of my life, I was helping with the picking when all but two of my uncles had to leave.

My Uncle Mike placed me directly behind the steering wheel. My feet couldn't reach the floor pedals so I sat on my crossed legs. He then put the truck in its extra low gear, and told me to drive it straight down the field while he, and my Uncle Joe, walked along side the slow moving truck lifting the crates and setting them onto the flat body. I could just about see above the steering wheel, but I held it as tight as I could, and made it all the way to the end of the field. Uncle Mike hopped in and turned it around to head back into the field to gather another row of crates. Back and forth we went slowly moving across the entire field. We finished the last row just as night dropped its dark curtain around the potato field. I rode on the back of the truck with the crates while Uncle Mike drove the truckload back to the sweet potato house where each crate would restfully sleep during its autumn and winter storage.

The building was mostly empty, and my interior fort was no longer available for me to play in. Doesn't matter, I thought, I'd build another fort in there sometime during the following summer after all these potatoes were sold off.

*   *   *

Somehow we all knew when it was time to play baseball. The World Series was played at the end of summer back then, and no one ever worried about having playoff games in icy cold weather. Each sport had its own season of the year. Baseball played the most games during the summer season, of course, because summer, we all thought, was about as long as the other three seasons put together.

The last time we played a game over on the real baseball field next to Kupenski's Bar, Ricky had cracked my bat while hitting, what seemed to me, a mile-long home run right over his brother Anthony's head, and into the deer woods behind the outfield. My father helped me squeeze the split baseball bat together using the vise in the garage shop. He drove three wood screws into the cracked bat, and then taped it all over using the black electrical wire tape. It hardly made the bat any heavier, and best of all, it didn't break again for the rest of the summer. The following Christmas, I got a new baseball bat, and so did Ricky. We couldn't believe it, but Billy got one too. There was no need for the once injured, but now healed bat. I put it into our yard shed expecting to have to use it when we broke one of the newer baseball bats, but Ricky never hit a ball as hard, or as far again. I don't recall ever breaking another baseball bat during our Milway summer series of what we called, the world competitions.

I re-wrapped one old baseball with fresh new electrical tape making it slick and harder to throw straight. We only had two baseballs, so, like everything else we had, we either repaired it, or did without it. You cannot play baseball without a ball.

Nearly all the kids around Milway showed up when we played baseball. Maybe some of the other guys might have contacted their neighbors saying what time we'd start the ball game the next day, but I never did. For me, it seemed that people just appeared. It was just another example of Milway's magic. The kids just appeared.

After the game, we'd all buy a soda at my uncle's bar, and then we'd sit under the row of Maple trees along the first base side of the field. Saint Mary's church held a big chicken bar-b-que there each year, and there were sections of the stands that remained all year long to be reused. We'd drink Canada Dry Ginger Ale if it were a really hot day; otherwise Black Cherry Wishniak and Orange Soda were our top selections.

We could play stickball anywhere, and as few as two guys could make up a team. When we had an odd number of people playing, I always liked being on the team with the one less person so I could get to bat more often. It was simple logic.

On exceptionally hot days, just Ricky, Billy, and I created the only motion of activity in town. When it was blistering outside, only Billy and I continued our normal routines. The very next day was an example of a real scorcher. During the morning, the two of us had planned to play marbles, but we shot our slingshots instead. That worked out very well for me because Billy got to be very good at shooting marbles, and had we played, I might have lost some of my favorite marbles, my blue cat-eyes. By early afternoon, with the sun burning down on us, the only place that made any sense was the cave.

*　　　*　　　*

Billy crawled in first. He found the box of wooden matches that Ricky had left there, lit two of the five candles we now had in place against the wall farthest from the entrance, and waited for me to enter. I had crawled into the dead-end tunnel on purpose just to check it out. Everything was fine. I worked myself backwards to the fork, and then scurried into the full cave. Billy was staring at a really large gray spider sitting near the candles.

"Look at the size of this bugger," he said.

"Biggest spider I've ever seen," I answered.

" Kill it."

"No, it's the first bug we've seen come in here," I told him. "There must be other smaller bugs around. He'd only come in here if he thought he could find something to eat."

"I don't like it."

"Me either."

"Kill it then."

"Okay, I told Billy, "but not until we're ready to leave. Let's see where it goes and what it'll do."

"Alright. But keep an eye on it."

We both moved across the cave to sit back and view the abnormally large gray spider. It looked like the venomous female funnel-web spider from Australia that I had read about. Female spiders are usually much larger than the males. All the men I knew were bigger than all the women I knew, and I was glad about that. It wouldn't be until many, many years later that I'd learn that females might be smaller than we guys are, but they're usually a lot smarter. They let *us* chase them, until *they* catch us. They didn't have to use webs.

I would read every night in my bed before falling asleep, so I was filled with thousands of bits of worthless information. I knew no spider could get to Milway from Australia, so this one must be a local Garden Orb Weaver, the *Neoscona crucifera* which is part of 2,800 similar species of spiders. They build large webs, then rest head downward, and wait for their prey. They are brightly colored on their stomachs, but neither Billy nor I were about to pick him up and turn him over. Instead we watched him slowly work his way toward the exit tunnel. That outside light sneaking softly in and caressing the orange gravel walls of our cave was distinctly different from any of our candle's light, which simply danced on the tip of the wick.

Billy and I discussed the large number of shooting stars we'd seen the night before. We talked about going back to the area in the woods where we'd planned to build the fort with a tree top lookout, but the memory of all the bee stings had left a lasting impression on his psyche, and I knew he'd learned that old adage about better being safe than sorry. The victorious bees had stopped that fort from ever being built.

We talked about riding our bikes to Kimble Bridge if it stayed this hot. We knew we could spend a lot of hours down there cooling off in the river, but we would end up soaking wet with sweat after the five mile bike ride back home. Then I said that it would be nice if the tiny stream, which was actually a drainage ditch over by the fire hall, were wider and deeper.

"Hey, that's a great idea," he said. "We dug this. We could dig a bigger area out and make our own pool area."

The most interesting ideas always seem to appear spontaneously. So do the completely impossible ideas.

We never enthusiastically began that project even though we did make one lethargic, lackluster effort at trying to create a wading area. We sat silently and stared at the hole we were in, and thought about all the work it took to make this cave. It was on dry land, and no water washed more dirt back into it as we dug it out. No, we thought, it may be a great idea to have a local pool area for Sahara-like days, but no one wanted to participate in all the labor it would take. I thought we were getting lazier. Maybe we were getting smarter, but if so, we never noticed it. I had an important question that needed an answer, and looked around to see if I could find Time spying on us. He would know. I hoped we weren't just getting older.

15-A

Tudor had to put in extra time whenever his father wasn't feeling well, so he worked more and more hours at the gas station. Anthony grew tired of we younger guys, and didn't take as many chances in our endeavors as he used to do just three months earlier. Philip and Jo-Jo still hung around, but only if we were playing one of our made-up games.

My brother Jimmy's older friends and he looked outward from Milway, and seldom joined in with any thing I was doing. None of the older guys were interested in make-believe conflicts as the center of their day's activities. My cousins, Gary and Billy, even my second cousin, Jackie, seldom worked on any of my late summer projects. They did like it when they could play some sporting events with us, but overall, they drifted away like the wind, from the chicken coops, forts, the hayloft, and even the farmland activities like planting or harvesting. They never came to the cave when I was there, but they knew they were welcome to visit anytime. Ricky would always be ready to help, but he too, had newer obligations and responsibilities at home. Billy, my neighbor, not my cousin, was all I had left to join me when I wanted to be free, totally free, from all the responsibilities that Time gets His cousin, Chance, to add to, and then complicate, our lives. I was still the King of the cave, and the Prince of the Milway. Time giggled as some premature element of autumn tried to sneak into our rye maze, our sports fields, and our nearby woods. We never noticed any of the autumn air visiting our back yards. It only swam by at sunrise, so we seldom smelled or heard it splashing through the bushes or tree limbs.

Autumn always approaches by riding in on the wingless wind from the northeast.

However, for now I was still the Count of the Chicken Coops even though we had one less building to occupy. I was still the Duke of the Barn, a lesser barn now that the cow and horse shed had been torn off it. My other Uncle Joe, not Popeye, Aunt Pauline's husband, could make his annual autumn wine, but I remained Prince of the Grapevines.

The one special activity Billy and I did repeat over and over again was when we'd lay out on my front lawn, beneath the towering spruce tree, and watch the summer stars blink Morse code messages to us. It was our responsibility to decipher their messages. They somehow affected the Milway of our youth. I can't read their messages anymore; I've outgrown the ability to do so. But even back then, just when we were nearly figuring out one of their distant Morse code messages, we'd be interrupted by the sound of Billy's mother calling that it was time to get home.

"Billy. Billy it's dark now, and time to get home," she called over the hedges, across the barnyard, and disrupted our scanning of the stars just when we were about to decipher one of their messages.

"On my way," was Billy's usual response to his mother's beckoning. Time too, would lie there quietly next to us thinking how

He came from that first enormous explosion; He was born in the Big Bang. His goofy brother, Luck, first came about when all the elements of the universe originally began to cluster themselves into planets, solar systems, and galaxies, when everything first accidently fell into place. Their first cousin, Chance, provided the spark that ignited life on our planet, and most likely, on thousands of the other tiny specks we could see in the sky.

Chance's job was to make everything that's totally insignificant develop some meaningful purpose on our tiny speck of dust on the edge of the Milky Way solar system among one billion other totally insignificant balls of dirt drifting through an infinity of open space.

Why I was aware of all this when I was only twelve is beyond me. Billy and I would look up, and ask questions about what it would be like to visit one of those bright shining fires in the sky, or at least get to one of the round rocks that circled them.

We were both sure that it would be some grownup who would do it first, and not either of us. We would never grow up. The stories about Peter Pan made the most sense to us. Chance had one younger sister, Joy, and an older sister named, Sorrow. It was Chance alone, with Time's permission, that would let you play with Joy when you were twelve, but she made you start spending more of your hours with Sorrow as you grew older. I could sense that Chance had sent Her older, bigger sister, Sorrow, to hang around my mother everyday since my grandmother had died. I wondered just how long my mother would keep Her around as an unwanted houseguest?

Chance accidently taught me that the only meaningful things are those activities that you alone deem important. Both bubbly Joy, and serious Sorrow, and their middle sister, Chance, were obligated to follow whatever that nitwit, Luck, commanded, but Time, yes Time, was in charge of them all, and He always had the last say in everything.

No matter what task I and my friends were working on, or whatever game we were playing, when I had to leave to deliver my newspapers, all my buddies accepted the fact that we were finished for the day. They respected my obligations, and I respected all the support they gave me. There were a lot of unwritten rules in Milway, and we followed them all.

16

After my grandmother had passed away, I fully understood that she wasn't going to be across the street from me anymore. I knew I'd never see her again, and I'd have to watch out for attacking chickens all by myself. She was gone forever, but death has no place to dwell in any part of a young boy's mind. There's simply no room for it.

My grandfather had turned ninety-nine years old just before my summer vacation had begun. He still walked to his shop in the barn every so often during the spring of that year, and even at the start of June, but by the end of July, I hadn't seem him around anywhere. I was amazed everyday when we were constructing our cave that he didn't come out to stop us from invading one of his better pieces of farmland.

None of the guys had any idea that my mother had checked out what we were doing. She then had a few of the younger men of Milway look it over. Every one of them told her that if the roof caved in, we could be buried alive under loads of Milway dirt. When she told me what the grownups were saying about the cave, I told her that I thought everybody, sooner or later, gets covered up with their local dirt. Having been an altar boy for a few years by then, I had served at a number of funeral Masses, and had become callous to the entire procedure. I thought the Vikings took care of their dead the right way. Cremation. I sometimes played at being a

Viking instead of playing Robin Hood. I was trying to make a joke about the dirt, but my mother simply didn't absorb my humor.

*   *   *

Ricky wanted nothing to do with any more digging, but Billy and I did go and scout out the tiny stream running by the firehouse. It ran toward McDonald Avenue, the road that we used to get to the old gravel pit where we had played Army with homemade mortars and firecrackers. From there, the little creek ran south through the deer woods all the way to Dorothy. In the swamp behind my Uncle Foxy's place, it widened to nearly six feet, and continued to get wider and deeper along its journey all the way to the town of *Tuckahoe*. The Lenape Indians, back in the 1600's, call that area a place where deer run freely, and Tuckahoe was their word for that expression, Tuckahoe. That little ditch of flowing water was the headwaters of the Tuckahoe River, which ran into the bay behind Ocean City and Somers Point. It was only two and a half feet wide where it started near the Milway Fire Hall, and expanded to about four feet wide where the water came from out from under McDonald Avenue through a large pipe with a three-foot diameter. From there, it continued to widen all the way to the sea. I used to think that even the Mississippi River had to start somewhere as a little trickle of water, maybe a flow no bigger than what we had in Milway. Everything starts small, and then grows into something big. Even people. I wondered if Maple Grove, Minnesota, where a tiny stream flows from a small lake and starts the Mississippi River, was anything like Milway?

Billy and I had one short shovel with us. I used it to dig into the riverbank just west of the Protestant Church and across the street from the Milway Fire Hall. It was a spot we checked out everyday when we were walking to school. We saw it nearly dry, and also viewed it flowing swiftly after a heavy rain; we even saw it frozen-over during the winter. We knew it quite well.

Billy picked up some of the fallen limbs lying in the water, and for about half an hour, we thought it might work, We'd have a wider, deeper place to cool off on really hot days without going all the way to Kimble Bridge that was miles and miles away. We knew we'd never be able to swim in it, but we could maybe get it to be deep enough to wade in, and wide enough to splash about, at least splash each other. I said that he should try digging out the side of the bank where he was standing. He took the shovel, tried to get one full shovelful, but the water washed all the soil away as he tried to dig. He quickly gave up. I agreed with his withdrawal, and we both conceded defeat. We had already learned from all our adventures into the woods, and into fields around Milway that Nature always wins. You have to pick your projects very carefully.

Billy saw it as a failure, as he carried the shovel over his handlebars, biking his way back to his house. I viewed it as something that we just didn't want badly enough. We wanted a cave. We made a cave. We played in the cave. There's something about doing less when summer's shadows grow longer, when too many minutes of daylight have disappeared, and sadly, you never noticed it happening. Neither the energy, nor the will, were there to change the course of the tiny creek. We left it alone for some other kids to modify, some kids who never dug a cave, some future boys who would never know how hard it was going to be, but would attempt and complete it anyway.

Later that evening, we all gathered at Spitz's gas station just to hang out. Stickball, tag, even Kick-the-Can was not on our agenda. Maybe there were a few games remaining on the pinball machine? I hoped so. Maybe somebody found a firecracker? Billy would love that. Ricky was the last one to arrive and he looked ill.

"What's the matter, Ricky?" I asked.

"You sick or something?" Billy added.

"Not really sick," Ricky answered. " Had to go to Vineland today with my mother and, well, you'll never believe it"

"Go on," I demanded.

"Well, right there on the first table you see in Newberry's were backpacks, notebooks, and boxes of pencils."

"No way!" exclaimed Billy.

"You're kidding," I added. "You've got to be kidding."

School stuff. School had to be a hundred years away. School wasn't something you even thought about when you're immersed in absolute total freedom. Had Time played a trick on us? No, we refused to believe it. I knew we had to change the subject before we all became ill-looking like Ricky, so I said, "Come on, let's see if they left anything where they tore down your chicken coop, Billy."

The danger of returning to a place where we've already had a catastrophe might add some excitement to our depression. There's just no way, we thought, that returning to school could ever be so near. Our good friend Time would never play a trick like that on us. Returning to the site where rusty nails captured and held our buddy, wasn't as frightening as the thought of having to return to a classroom where we'd be forced to give up the freedom of making our own decisions about what we'd do each day.

The entire coop was now demolished, and all the wooden frames, roofing, and metal chicken bins had been removed. Back at my house, the barn still stood, but the section along side it where there was once a cow, even a horse when I was much younger, were also torn down, cleaned up, and changed forever.

This was the time of the year when my uncles used to butcher some of the hogs that were kept behind my grandfather's place. But he was too old to do it now, and his children, my uncles, didn't want to bother anymore. "It's easier to just buy all the ham or pork you want," my Uncle Popeye said when I asked him about why we didn't raise pigs any more?

We found nothing around the vanished chicken coop that we might incorporate into some new game we'd invent. We returned to the garage, but there wasn't even one free game remaining to be played on the pinball machine. We all walked quietly back to our homes as the black blanket of night was pulled up and tucked in around our part of the world.

We all went to sleep that night with an uneasy feeling. We knew how a convicted criminal must feel just before he was carried off to be incarcerated, relinquishing all his freedom.

"Just our luck," said Billy just as he was leaving for his house. "They might start school sooner than usual."

They didn't start early, and Billy had no idea that Luck had been hanging around with us since the end of May even though He and Billy hadn't been very good friends. Sure, Luck was a dimwit, and his brother, Time, kept an eye on him, but it just wasn't fair when neither of them let us know they were lurking around in our neighborhood.

The next morning, Billy and I rode our bicycles down Tuckahoe Road to check out Foxy's old house way out in the woods behind Kupin's farm. Mr. Kupin had only one son, and a whole covey of girls. Nancy was just one year older than us if you're counting years, but she was ten years older than all of us in maturity. We played together in school, but she never participated in anything our all-boy's gang was doing.

We rode past Dexter's house, then up Mr. Kupin's long driveway into the woods. We turned left, and then biked another three-quarters of a mile to the once productive ten-acre farm. It was a long ride through nothing but woods. The fields around the ancient homestead were over-grown with tall weeds; only the block foundations remain of what once was a barn and a chicken coop. They were sad reminders of what there once was. Only the two-story clapboard house was left. Uncle Foxy didn't do anything with the place; he just owned it after the young couple that settled there, and cleared and farmed the land in the late 1800's, gave it up, and then left after they grew too old to work it. We loved how quiet it was whenever we were down there. Many years later, when that two-story house, built over a stone root cellar, finally collapsed, my Uncle Joe, and my Uncle Mike, built a hunting club on the site. The club building was simply a roof built over the ancient cellar foundation that was constructed with some red bricks and Jersey sandstone. Standing outside of it, you could touch the highest peak of the roof. They put in a wood-burning stove, and some bunk beds. It was very primitive, but hunting itself is a very primitive sport stemming from what was once a survival necessity.

I would hunt deer from that location for the next fifty years harvesting over 160 deer myself. That broke my father's deer-kill record of 155. My father hunted with Mr. Kupin's brother, Andy. Only God knows how many deer Andy brought down. He never wasted a bit of them. Andy survived on venison.

The original house was still standing on that late summer day when we arrived, so Billy and I scouted out the root cellar, and checked out the first floor. Like the root cellar, it was empty except for one old kitchen chair. We only made one or two visits a year down there, and we never expected to find anything. Just being there was like being in the distant past. For us, time traveling was real. I felt that, but couldn't explain it to Billy. We then made a sweeping walk all around the ten acres of grassy abandoned fields pointing out the deer trails and rabbit paths. As soon as we returned to our bikes, we headed back toward home. We stopped, like we always did, at Dexter's to hand pump a refreshing drink of well water. Dexter wasn't home, but we were always welcome to stop in for a drink.

I told Billy the story my mother told me about Foxy's place. She said that when she was a very young girl, even younger than I was right now, she'd help her mother in the small grocery story that was part of her house. It was the same house that my grandparents lived in directly across the street from my house. My house was right next to the field with the cave in it. The couple that first settled and built Foxy's place would ride to the center of town each Saturday with a horse and buggy. They always shared a penny candy with her. It all seemed to me like an old western story from the Roy Rodgers television show. I couldn't picture any of it happening in Milway. I couldn't picture my mother ever being a little girl. Grownups, we thought, had always been grown up. I had strong reservations about the validity of her story.

*   *   *

We got back to my house just in time to see my family's friend, Tony Merkeysly, using his backhoe to fill in our cave. My heart pumped faster and I'm certain that Billy could hear it. While we were searching an abandoned house, Tony was following my mother's instructions to destroy the cave, and prevent anything bad from happening to us. We were really upset about it. Tony told us that he buried every part of the roof lumber inside, then scraped all the dirt we'd shoveled out back into the cave, and refilled the entire entrance tunnel. Tudor's flashlight was laid to rest with everything else that was in there. Tony said that he'd never seen anything like it. "That could have been the cellar of a regular house," he told us. "Course, if it fell in on ya, you'd all die," he added.

As the sun dipped to touch the tree line around Milway, nothing was left of our cave, the biggest project of our lifetime, but a mound of dirt over the far part of a weed-covered field. Anytime you dig a hole, and then try to refill it, you end up with what seems like more dirt than you took out. That's because the original dirt was tightly packed down. The mound above a grave will settle over the following years just as the mound over our cave would settle down in the years to come. Today, it's impossible to tell where the biggest cave in Milway, maybe in all of South Jersey, had ever been. We were saddened, but not angry. My mother really thought we might get seriously hurt, even killed, in the confines of that cave. As the days shortened, and the fiery summer days cooled off a bit, all the other guys had stopped visiting the cave. Billy and I were the only ones still using it and continued to hide from a cooler sun under the earth. Only he and I would really miss it, and I was certain that I was the most disappointed.

"Should we dig another one someplace else?" Bill inquired as we dropped off our bikes in my back yard, and walked over to the now defunct cave site.

"No," I answered him. "We'd never have enough time before we have to go back to school. It'll never be the same." Besides, there are some miraculous things in life that can never be repeated, and that's good. It's what makes those few special events life-long memories. Everything that's repeatable, slowly, but easily, slips out of your mind. Take a vacation to the same place more than once, and you only recall the most recent trip. It's good that you only get the chance to do some things once. I can see how Chance was such a close relative of Time and Luck; their first cousin in fact. Don't miss your chance to do the things you want to do or visit the places you'd like to see, my father used to tell me. Yes, Time prevented Chance from making many return visits to our neighborhood. She had other boys to see. We were only twelve, but we already knew that.

*   *   *

The following afternoon, my mother left a pan of Polish Pierogies for my father and me to heat up for dinner. She was across the street all evening, but she had made the Polish dumplings filled with potatoes and cheese much earlier, and had them ready for us to eat. Maybe, I thought, she had made them to remind her of what she so often had made for her own father, or what her mother had made for her. They were already boiled, so all we had to do was warm them up in a frying pan, and add some sizzling butter to make them golden brown. During dinner, my father asked if I'd like to go flounder fishing out on the Delaware Bay. "Yes," I told him. "When?"

"Maybe next Saturday. We'll see how everything goes," he retorted. My father loved to fish. He learned how while still a young boy in Ireland, and he still enjoyed fishing better than anything else he did, except maybe to go deer hunting.

He said nothing at all as we ate about what was going on across the street at my grandfather's house. I'd have to wait until I woke up the following morning before I was given any information about the buzz of activity that had been taking place over there.

It was my brother Jimmy who first said, "Grandpop George died last night."

"Gee," was all I answered.

"You know he'd been very sick for a while."

"I haven't seen him around anywhere," I affirmed acknowledging that I was aware of his absence from everywhere I'd been playing.

"It hasn't been that long since Grandmom Anna died. He was ninety-nine years old. Did you know that?"

I didn't answer his question about my grandfather's age. "I guess when you've been with somebody a long, long time, you miss them even more than if you were with somebody for just a short time," I tried to philosophize.

"Mom said he just gave up. Since Grandmom died, he hasn't said anything, or eaten very much. Remember, he was too sick to go to her funeral."

"How's mom?" I asked.

"She's arranging everything. She's busy. She doesn't have time right now to think about anything else."

This was only the second death that I was aware of, not counting when my hound dog, Elmer, died. Counting Elmer's demise, Death had only made three visits to me. We all know that it takes a repetition of three to make a complete impact on you, or record something permanently on the pages of nerves in the library of your mind.

Elmer's demise was two years ago when I was ten. Elmer had caught some disease, and everyone said it would kill him. They all said it would be better for him if we shot him, put him down, was the phrase they said, and took him out of his misery. I didn't want him to be in pain, and I didn't want him to die. It seems that Chance gave me the opportunity to do something for him, but in doing it, I would feel the pain instead of him.

I remember I didn't want to do anything until my father said Elmer was getting sicker, and that he was in lots of pain. We had to end it, I was certain, after I spent a day looking into his sad, sad eyes. So, my brother and I took him in the pickup down to the gravel pits, dug a large hole, and then Jimmy took out our 22 rifle from behind the truck seat. I said that I wanted to give him a piece of candy, and tried to put it in his mouth, but Elmer was too sick to even taste it.

"Okay," Jimmy said, "he's your dog. Put him down."

He gave me instructions as to where to shoot so it would be quick and painless. I didn't want to do it, but I did. One shot, right behind his right ear. He instantly dropped, even before the echo of the shot faded away. All his pain was gone. I remember feeling it soaking into me.

We buried him and drove home without saying anything, not a single word to each other. I hated my brother for making me do it myself, but in retrospect, I came to realize that if he had done it, I would have hated him for shooting Elmer. It made me accept a kind of grownup responsibility. It made me grow up a little faster, but I didn't ever want to grow up. Looking back on the episode, I'm glad he let me be responsible for Elmer.

Counting Elmer, it took three deaths for me to realize Death was another character, also born from the Big Bang, and while most people think He's the same as Time, He's not. Time had kept Him away from my Grandfather for ninety-nine years.

Back at my house on the day my grandfather died, while sitting on our front steps looking across the street toward my grandparent's place, just behind where Billy and I would lie on the grass and study the stars, my brother, Jimmy, said something that I understood right away. In an instant, I knew Luck may or may not like you; Chance provides you opportunities; Time is always hanging around, and spying on you, but Death never stops working. He never takes a rest. He makes the autumn leaves fall; He encourages you to swat flies; He helps older birds push the baby bird out of its over-crowded nest, and He waits to come visit everyone of us.

"You know," Jimmy said to me as I sat on those front steps, quietly worrying about my mother, "this means we just moved up a full generation."

Without personally knowing the strange characters whom I often thought about that came from the Big Bang, my brother pointed out that my parents were next in line, and after that, we too would be abandoned by Luck, ignored by Chance, and have Time permit his mysterious colleague to take control of it all. I knew that he had no idea what an impact his words had on me. I understood everything that he told me. He would soon join the Navy, and then leave Milway forever, but I planned to take advantage of every minute Time would provide. I'd make sure Billy and I filled every day with wonder and adventure. When I had to put down my sick dog, Elmer, I just did it. There was no contemplation about his existence ending. Even when I learned that my Grandmother had passed away, I realized that I wouldn't see her anymore, but I was just twelve, and consequences of life have different interpretations, unique elucidations, at that age. However, for some totally unknown reason, after my Grandfather died, and my brother explained that he and I had just moved up a full generation, I had an epiphany, a realization, a sting of maturity, that only grownups were suppose to experience. I was haunted by the fact that I had become a different kind of twelve. I wasn't the same twelve-years-old that I had been yesterday. I realized that everything comes to an end, even the infinity I knew as summer. I knew that my parents, and all my aunts and uncles, even Ricky and Billy, and our entire gang, along with Jimmy and even me, would have to journey into that good night. Time's numbskull brother. Luck, hadn't prevented this realization from happening to me. I was angry because I understood.

*   *   *

I felt as though summer had picked up speed, and was starting to fly past me. I wanted some peaches for dessert that night, and even though winter was still far away, my mother opened a fresh quart jar; she and I each ate half of the entire Mason jar of peaches filled with sunshine that had been here a full month ago. I remembered seeing the rays dancing from leaf to leaf in the peach orchard.

Each golden sweet peach slice was filled with the sunshine of the day when I built a fort, played Kick-the-Can, climbed up the hayloft with Jimbo and then jumped down into a hay pile that hid a pitchfork. During my brief life, besides hearing my family and friends talking, I was certain I had overheard Chance and Luck quarreling over many of the things I was doing. Their voices weren't just in my head. No, I could hear them calling out through the same grass I played on, the same trees I climbed, and in the air moving past my ears as I rode my bike.

Another slice was filled with the heat from when we started to dig our cave. A different slice held the rays of light that were exposed on the day I went to Kimble Bridge with my New York cousins. My mother said very little but taught me so much. I think she knew I had come to understand some new things about grownup life, and she tried to tell me not to explain it all to my buddies. She said that they'd have to learn all the most important things by themselves. Nothing else was said out loud that evening. I was afraid that I could never be twelve again, something that I wanted to be forever. Time sent everyone away except Chance's older sister. We sat silently and finished eating the quart jar of peaches.

Besides the sunshine, the peaches in each quart had also captured a tiny piece of Time, and sealed a fraction of Him up until we alone wanted to release Him. That we did. On so many future frozen winter nights, we released the golden summer sunshine that my mother and I had captured in July. All it took to do it was opening another quart jar of peaches.

POSTSCRIPT

The peach. Its scientific name, *persica* was modified into a number of languages all across Europe. It derives from the understanding that peaches came from Persia, our modern day Iran. During their empire, the Romans called the fruit *malum persiocum*, or Persian apple. When Latin degraded into French, it was called pêche; that's where the English got their word *peach*. The full scientific name *Prunus persica*, simply means "Persian plum".

In Korea, the peach is the featured symbol of happiness and longevity. It is a "good luck" fruit for prosperity.

This peach symbol of Longevity is many times used on birthday cakes and drawn onto birthday cards. It is one of the three blessed fruits in Buddhism.

The Japanese use the peach to symbolize truth, and it, many times, is depicted as the Tree of Life. Their legend of *Izanaki* highlights the protective power of the peach as he defeats the gods of thunder when he throws three peaches into their stance.

The peach, according to the Taoists, is the elixir of life, and they show, *Shouskin*, the god of longevity, with a peach in his hand. In other Chinese mythology, immortality is obtained from *xian-tao*, the peach. The tree itself is associated with a unique protective magic, and amulets and talismans carved from the wood of peach trees were thought to be helpful safeguards against malicious spirits.

The peach is native to China, and peach pits over 7,000 years old have been found in northwestern parts of China and Tibet. Over the centuries, the tree was transported to the Middle East, where the Romans sampled it and then took it home and spread it around Europe.

In Egypt, the peach is dedicated to their ancient god, *Harpokrat*, the morning sun, and eating a peach in the morning aided in a long life.

Many famous artists painted still life pieces with peach fruit as their key object. Caravaggio, Renoir, Campi, Monet, Manet, Fantin-Latour, Roesen, Rubens, and Van Gogh all provide excellent examples of the importance of the peach as an artistic symbol. In Jan van Eyck's "The Arnolfini Marriage" the symbolic peaches are on the table, almost out of sight, but highly symbolic.

The peach has long been the symbol of youth and immortality. Peach flowers reflect softness, purity, and peace.

John Mahoney was born in Milmay, New Jersey and is an alumnus of LaSalle University. As an undergraduate, he spent his summers working on a construction crew, learning his father's trade while earning money for school.

John is the author of eight books, including three collections of poetry, and is a long-time food and wine columnist. A lifelong educator, he is a respected scholar of Shakespeare and Chaucer who has taught at the high school and university level. A former New Jersey Freeholder and candidate for the United States Congress, John is now best known as an internationally recognized wine expert having written three books on wine.

Made in the USA
Monee, IL
14 March 2020